Hiring for Fit

Hiring for Fit

A Key Leadership Skill

Janet Webb

BEP BUSINESS EXPERT PRESS

First published in 2020 by
Business Expert Press, LLC
222 East 46th Street, New York, NY 10017
www.businessexpertpress.com

ISBN-13: 978-1-95152-754-9 (paperback)
ISBN-13: 978-1-95152-755-6 (e-book)

Business Expert Press Human Resource Management and Organizational Behavior Collection

Collection ISSN: 1946-5637 (print)
Collection ISSN: 1946-5645 (electronic)

Cover image licensed by Ingram Image, StockPhotoSecrets.com
Cover and interior design by S4Carlisle Publishing Services Private Ltd., Chennai, India

First edition: 2020

10 9 8 7 6 5 4 3 2 1

Printed in the United States of America.

Advanced Quotes for *Hiring for Fit*

I would highly recommend this book for anyone in a management role that needs to recruit top talent aligned to their company's goals. *Hiring for Fit* provides a system to ensure that leaders have the knowledge and foundation required to make great hires and retain them. The Trait Alignment Protocol (TAP) system outlined in the book is a pragmatic, results-oriented approach that ensures leaders understand and recruit the right fit for all positions.

Kim Hannan, CHRL
Vice President Talent & Culture
Cole Engineering Group

Hiring the right people for the right positions is an art ... and Janet's book sheds light on how to do it right the first time. Having led teams in different parts of the world, Janet's book addresses the most important piece of the puzzle—*Hiring for Fit*. It is a great read for global business leaders.

Eric Wong, CPA, CA
Vice-President, Hospitality, Asia Pacific
Infor Hospitality

As an employment lawyer, I assist employers on a daily basis to deal with employment issues that arise as a result of hiring the wrong person. While not "Hiring for Fit" gives employment lawyers work, it can be very costly for employers, not only financially but also in terms of business productivity, employee morale, and wasted resources. This book provides a comprehensive guide to employers on how to hire the right person from the start so they can avoid the legal and other negative consequences that result when they don't!

Carita Wong, LL.B.
Partner, Israel Foulon LLP
Employment and Labour lawyer

Hiring for Fit provides actionable guidance in making great hiring decisions. Janet takes you through a structured process that clarifies the meaning of fit and how to find it. And the book's "Fit in Action" stories and tips to avoid hiring pitfalls are very relatable. By applying Janet's proven approach, I avoided what might be considered a safer "same-to-same" type candidate and selected a bright, curious person from another industry who was an excellent hire. The "Hiring-for-Fit" approach provides me the structure to support better decisions that repeatedly result in excellent long-term hires, and it will help you too!

Jim O'Neill, CPA, CA, Acc.Dir.
CFO of public and private companies operating internationally

Hiring for Fit is a great resource for navigating the challenge of recruiting successfully, where hiring failures are costly in monetary terms, to employee morale, and, ultimately, to business purpose. If you're responsible in any way for hiring, having this guide to hand and referring to it over and over again will surely mitigate the risk of falling into the trap of hiring only for apparent technical compatibility and not paying enough attention to the right soft skills that play such a significant part in building great teams and providing excellent service, whatever industry you're in.

Lisa S. Becker, FCA
Chief Operating Officer
University of Toronto Asset Management Corporation

Janet Webb's *Hiring for Fit* is an exceptional guide for business leaders to acquire and retain top talent, and the approach has a proven record of success. I personally found the information about fit traits to be instrumental in hiring successfully, from assessing soft skills to ensuring cultural fit!

Penny Galanis
Senior Director, Employee Experience
Broader Public Sector of Ontario

Abstract

A key skill for any leader is the ability to hire a great team, and this skill requires a considerable depth of knowledge of the complex subject of fit. Most organizations talk about the need to hire for fit, but many go about hiring in the wrong way because their leaders don't fully understand the concept of fit. The results are poor performance and unnecessary and costly turnover.

Hiring for Fit goes to the heart of what fit really means and provides expert insight for anyone involved in making hiring decisions. In over 30 years of experience in executive search and career management, Janet Webb has studied the personality traits and attributes of successful hires in a wide range of roles and has developed a system to hire the right fit for any role. This system recognizes that each role is unique and requires specific traits for success. The entire process outlined in the book, from identifying and screening top talent to onboarding new hires and supporting the development of senior leaders, is an application of Janet Webb's unique Trait Alignment Protocol (TAP), which is the key to identifying fit and maintaining fit over the long term.

The book provides leaders with practical steps they can follow to apply fit successfully in the hiring process and explains the meaning of fit, how to develop the job description into a position profile that incorporates fit requirements for each specific organization and role, how to structure the hiring process to determine fit, and how to interview candidates to reveal genuine fit with the job and the organization. The book also details steps for maintaining a focus on fit after the hire by providing strategies for onboarding, performance reviews, retention, career development, and succession planning.

In addition, the book contains a Hiring-for-Fit Checklist, which is a tool for monitoring adherence to the key steps in applying TAP in hiring for fit, and a chapter on how to avoid common hiring pitfalls. Each chapter includes a "Fit in Action" feature with examples from real-life hiring challenges.

By applying the thorough and practical fit strategy described in the book, leaders will gain expertise in the complex subject of fit; replace seat-of-the-pants hiring with a reliable process; gain confidence in assessing a candidate's fit; make well-founded hiring decisions that avoid common hiring pitfalls; and pave the way for employee retention, promotions, and succession planning that add to the bottom line.

Keywords

fit; hiring; leadership; interviewing; soft skills; recruiting; screening; candidates; employees; organizational culture; personality; performance reviews; retention; succession planning; talent; traits; job description

Contents

Acknowledgments

I am grateful for the opportunity to work with such a wide range of clients, in executive search, management consulting, outplacement, and career and business coaching. Their numerous questions regarding the challenges of ensuring the "right fit" gave rise to the writing of this book.

I would like to thank Business Expert Press for providing expertise and guidance throughout all stages of the publishing process.

I would also like to acknowledge contributions from the following members of my team:

Mike Webb for his thorough review, input, and editorial consulting and development
Bruce McDougall for his input and editorial suggestions
Louise Rossi-Chan for review and helpful feedback
Jane Maguire for cover design consulting
David Chang for author photograph

And, finally, my thanks go to Natale Fiumara and Beryl Maguire for their love and support.

Disclaimer

The information and resources contained in this book are provided as is. Please note that this guide is based on extensive personal experience acquired in executive search, management consulting, outplacement, and career and business coaching. Nothing in this book is intended to replace common sense or legal or other professional advice. The author, Janet Webb, assumes no responsibility for errors or omissions, does not provide any warranty or guarantee, and cannot be held liable for the actions of those who purchase this book.

Also, you should use this information as you see fit. Your particular situation may not be exactly suited to the examples illustrated here; in fact, it's likely that it won't be. You should use your judgment to adjust your use of the information and recommendations to your particular situation. We sincerely hope that your use of this information will transform your approach to hiring and will result in increased success in your hiring practices.

Introduction

Because of the significant costs involved in hiring and training staff, every organization needs to increase its rate of success in hiring productive employees and reducing unnecessary staff turnover. In my experience, this increased success depends on hiring for fit.

In over 30 years of leading executive search, management consulting, outplacement, career coaching, and business coaching services, my focus has been on understanding fully the concept of fit from both the employer's and the candidate's perspectives. I've incorporated my expertise into the search processes at my company, JW Associates International Inc., to help hiring managers understand and apply the concept of fit. While this book addresses the employer's approach to the hiring process, it can also help individual professionals understand the importance of fit in advancing their careers.

Who Should Read This Book?

Everyone involved in the hiring process needs a clear understanding of the concept of fit, from company presidents looking for C-level staff, to midlevel managers seeking specialist employees, to HR managers hiring for their employers, and to recruiters working on behalf of their clients. This book addresses this need by explaining the concept and providing a step-by-step guide to hiring for fit. I've written this book for two distinct groups of readers:

Hiring Managers at All Levels

Whether you're a manager, director, vice president, C-level executive, president, or company owner, it's likely that hiring isn't your key focus. Consequently, you may conduct a search only occasionally. Additionally, you may work in a company without experienced HR specialists to support you. This book will help you understand more clearly the importance of hiring for fit and show you how to apply this understanding in an organized approach to successful recruitment.

HR Professionals and Recruiters

For HR professionals and recruiters familiar with the concept of fit in general terms, this book will provide additional insight into the process of hiring for fit. It will also provide a useful tool for explaining the importance of fit to hiring managers and for ensuring that everyone involved in the hiring process uses a consistent approach and applies agreed-upon search criteria.

The Challenge of Determining Fit

In its simplest form, *fit is the compatibility of the candidate with the role and with the employer.* A typical search begins with hiring managers identifying the hard skills they require in a candidate. These are the transferable skills, acquired through the development of technical or professional expertise and through specific work experience, required to perform well in a particular role. Organizations can usually articulate these required hard skills clearly and precisely.

The real challenge begins in defining the soft skills required for the job. I find that very few clients can clearly articulate in detail the important personal qualities that an individual needs to succeed in a specific role or to become a long-term asset to the organization. "I want an A-player with strong interpersonal skills," they say. But what does this really mean, and does it go far enough in setting a basis for fit? From over 30 years of executive search and career management experience, I'm convinced that the answer is "no."

To find a candidate with a good fit, you need the tools to screen for the broader aspects of it. Otherwise, you may spend valuable time and resources on hiring a candidate with only the necessary hard skills, to discover later that the new hire really doesn't fit the personal requirements of the role or the dynamics of the organizational culture.

In my experience as an outplacement provider, I find that organizations seldom dismiss an individual because of a lack of hard skills. Almost invariably, the individual who's let go is seen as lacking the necessary soft skills. Unfortunately, few organizations inform individuals about the specific soft skills they need to develop to excel in their roles. Instead, dismissed individuals hear only the puzzling news that they are "not the right fit."

This book explains how soft skills determine an individual's chances of success in an organization and in a specific role and how hiring managers can identify these soft skills more precisely. By screening effectively for the soft skills required, you can identify the individual who will become a great fit in the role and a successful long-term employee with the potential to grow in your organization.

At the end of each chapter, I've included a "Fit in Action" feature as an example of how the concepts in the book have applied to real-life hiring challenges. These examples, drawn from numerous situations I've observed over the years, are all factually based. However, I've changed some details to protect the identities of employers, employees, and candidates.

CHAPTER 1

Are You about to Hire the Wrong Fit?

How Does Hiring the Wrong Fit Happen?

The conventional wisdom is that a person needs to spend 10,000 hours in a challenging pursuit to become accomplished. Yet most managers undertake a key part of their organization's success—the challenge of hiring the right employees—only occasionally. As a result, it's difficult for managers to acquire the knowledge, skills, or experience needed to assess a candidate's fit with much accuracy. Organizations hire candidates with the wrong fit for two main reasons:

1. Many interviewers rely on gut feel to assess a candidate's fit, with unreliable results. There's no question that instinct and intuition contribute to the assessment of a candidate, especially when backed by extensive experience in hiring. But even for experienced interviewers, gut feel has its limitations, and there's always the possibility that interviewers' personal bias may compromise their rational judgment. Instinct should play a secondary role in the assessment of a candidate and should never be the principal basis for determining fit.

2. Most interviewers primarily screen candidates according to the hard skills required for the role. They feel most comfortable asking questions about these hard skills, listening to candidates' answers, and analyzing this information. Some hiring managers have occupied the same role—or a similar role—themselves, have many of the same hard skills, and are adept at screening for them.

Organizations also emphasize hard skills in the written description of the role. For example, the job description and interviews for a Director of

Financial Reporting position may emphasize the candidates' knowledge of consolidations and accounting systems, and experience in report writing and staff management. But the typical screening process pays much less attention than necessary to the critical soft skills required for the job, such as the ability to forge relationships across the organization, assertiveness, responsiveness, and highly developed organizational skills.

For a Vice President (VP) of Operations role, the job description and interviews may emphasize such hard skills as demonstrated strategic leadership accomplishments, previous P&L responsibility, and experience in operations management and quality control. But the screening process may pay less attention to such soft skills as building trusted relationships with customers and suppliers, setting high expectations for quality, and providing clear direction to staff, all of which may be essential to success in the role.

The Huge Cost of Failing to Identify Fit

Organizations invest time, effort, and money in assessing and hiring new employees. To receive the maximum return on this investment, organizations need to ensure that a candidate has both the hard skills and the soft skills needed to fit into the specific role and the organizational environment. Unless an organization adequately screens candidates for both sets of skills, the performance of newly hired employees may suffer because of conflicts with their colleagues and setbacks in their working relationships.

The negative consequences of hiring a bad fit can extend far beyond the individual's effectiveness in a specific role. A bad fit can impose intolerable stress on other employees and diminish morale among the individual's key colleagues and direct reports. In extreme cases, strong performers may leave the organization as a result.

When organizations hire a bad fit, they often compound the impact by revising organizational structures to accommodate areas of dysfunction, rather than addressing the fit issue directly. While the measures taken may alleviate the immediate problem, the revised organizational structures may not work in the best interest of the organization itself. I've frequently encountered hiring managers who have retained long-term employees who don't fit within their organization. Ultimately, the organization may dismiss these long-term employees, but only after they wreak havoc on the productivity of the group.

Is Your Organization Vulnerable?

Organizations stand a much better chance of finding the right individual for a job if hiring managers articulate clearly from the outset the qualities that the job requires. In addition to the expertise and experience required for the job, such as finance skills or a background in marketing, organizations must specify the soft skills involved in doing the job well and in adapting to the new culture. These soft skills might reflect time-management ability, the ability to build rapport, and the capacity to work independently. (We will discuss soft skills in more detail in Chapters 2 and 3.) Organizations also need procedures in place so that everyone involved in screening candidates applies the same criteria and discusses each candidate's skills from a shared perspective.

Answering yes or no to the following five questions will help you see if you're already on the right track in establishing fit:

1. Can you name all the important soft skills needed to succeed in the role you're filling?
2. Within your organization, will everyone involved in screening and interviewing candidates look for these same soft skills?
3. Does the job description clearly incorporate these key soft skills into the functional responsibilities of the role, so that interviewers and candidates clearly understand its behavioral requirements?
4. Do you know how to prescreen candidates for soft-skill fit, how to set up, prepare for, and conduct an effective interview, and how to analyze each short-listed candidate's verbal responses, body language, and actions?
5. Does your organization have postinterview meetings to discuss and reach consensus on the soft skills of short-listed candidates?

If you answered "yes" to fewer than four of these questions, then you're probably relying on your gut feel rather than a clearly articulated framework to assess a job candidate's fit.

In subsequent chapters, we will discuss the key steps you need to take to improve your organization's track record in hiring for fit.

Fit in Action: Learning from Mistakes

One of my search clients told me that, several years earlier, his company had hired a poorly screened individual who was now adversely affecting the entire department. The organization had hired the employee for her technical skills but without sufficient regard to the soft-skill aspect of her fit. The hiring manager had screened the candidate for her specific job skills, which she possessed in abundance. The new employee "knew her stuff," my client said and looked as if she could get the job done well. But as she settled into her job, she began to miss deadlines. She revealed herself to have no concern for results, and she wouldn't ask for help when she needed it.

The company was still dealing with the ongoing repercussions. To stick to important schedules, the employee's manager asked her to alert him in advance if she didn't think she could meet an imminent deadline. The employee agreed to do this but submitted incomplete work when the next deadline arrived. Her manager reminded her that she had agreed to notify him if she couldn't finish a job on time. The employee said, "That's what I'm doing now. As you can see clearly, the job's not done!" Technically accomplished as she was, this employee fell far short of a good fit with regard to her attitude.

With proper screening, the organization could have avoided hiring a bad fit by identifying the candidate's soft-skill deficiencies during the search screening process, including her inadequate regard for results and lack of humility. But, unfortunately, the hiring manager had taken for granted that the candidate had the soft skills required for a good fit, including a strong work ethic, respect for others, resilience, and a focus on results.

CHAPTER 2

What Are Fit Traits?

In Chapter 1, we stressed the importance of considering both hard and soft skills in establishing fit and indicated the greater difficulty involved in ensuring the compatibility of soft skills. *One of the challenges that interviewers face is that they meet the candidate only in the atypical setting of an interview.* They never get to see the candidate in action in the workplace.

The interviewer's aim is to assess how well the candidate would work with key stakeholders in the organization, including their boss, their peers, and—for managerial roles—their staff. Some roles may also require candidates to establish productive working relationships cross-functionally or with external stakeholders. To assess the candidate's likely future performance, the interviewer must closely observe how the candidate behaves in the interview and then ask the question "how will they actually behave in this role in this organization?"

From many years of experience, I've developed a rigorous method that facilitates this assessment process and termed it the ***Trait Alignment Protocol,*** or *TAP.* The method depends on the use of observed behaviors to establish the traits of the candidate and on the comparison of those traits with the ones needed to succeed in the organization and in the role. Whereas **behaviors** are the ways in which one acts or conducts oneself, especially toward others, **traits** are the underlying distinguishing qualities or characteristics.

For example, a candidate whose behaviors include listening carefully to all interview questions and always responding thoughtfully and clearly is likely to have such traits as respect for others, ability to focus, responsiveness, and straightforwardness. Of course, interviewers must consider the evidence as a whole in drawing conclusions. Should the same candidate behave rudely or indifferently toward the receptionist prior to the interview, the candidate's apparent respect shown in the interview is more likely for show than an expression of a genuine trait.

When considering fit traits, it helps to separate them into two categories:

- **Fundamental traits** are characteristics needed for success *in any role* in your organization. They relate to personal values and compatibility with the corporate culture, values, and objectives.
- **Complementary traits** are characteristics needed for success *in a particular role* in your organization. They relate to the role-specific interpersonal, communication, and leadership skills required and can vary widely in complexity and sophistication for roles of different types at different levels of seniority.

Analyzing Fundamental Traits

We continually refine our methodology by monitoring the progress of successful candidates hired by our clients. Based on this information, we've analyzed the fundamental traits that contribute to a candidate's long-term career success. These key hiring traits remain remarkably consistent regardless of the role that the candidate is hired to fill in a particular organization. In our experience, when newly hired employees don't fit within an organization, they inevitably haven't been screened thoroughly for these fundamental traits. Given the frequency with which we see this problem, we regard screening for fundamental traits as an essential, yet often-overlooked, part of hiring for fit.

We find that fundamental traits can be grouped into the following five categories to cover the key areas that are measures of compatibility with an organization and requirements for success in any role within that organization.

1. **Productivity:** Is there evidence that the individual can get the job done?
2. **Self-management:** Is there evidence that the individual can control his or her emotions and actions?
3. **Building relationships:** Is there evidence that this person can work with others?
4. **Presentation:** Is there evidence of appropriate grooming, body language, and communication skills?
5. **Open mindset:** Is there evidence of a willingness to listen to the ideas of others?

Within each of these five categories, we can list a number of specific traits that contribute to success. In the examples below, each trait appears in just one category, although it may also affect the assessment of a candidate under another category. Dependability, for example, appears as a trait in the category of Productivity, but may also influence a candidate's self-management and building of relationships.

These examples aren't intended to be exhaustive, but, based on our experience, this list identifies the most common fundamental traits involved in assessing fit with an organization. (This list appears again as Supplement 2 at the end of the book so that you can refer to it easily as you begin the hiring process.)

Fundamental Traits List

Productivity

Accountability
Accuracy
Analytical ability
Can-do attitude
Commitment to quality
Decision-making ability
Dependability
Determination
Diligence
Efficiency
Hard-working approach
Logical mindset
Persistence
Responsibility
Responsiveness
Results-orientation
Thoroughness
Timeliness
Will to succeed
Work ethic

Self-management

Ability to balance work and rest
Ability to deal with stress
Ability to manage emotions
Calmness
Energy level
Focus
Follow-through
Integrity
Judgment
Organizational ability
Punctuality
Resilience
Respect for physical boundaries
Self-awareness
Self-control
Self-discipline
Self-respect
Time-management ability
Understanding one's impact on
    other

Relationship building
  Ability to build rapport
  Appreciativeness
  Cooperativeness
  Empathy
  Enthusiasm
  Fairness
  Friendliness
  Gratitude
  Helpfulness
  Honesty
  Humility
  Humor
  Interest in others
  Loyalty
  Patience
  Politeness
  Positive attitude
  Reasonableness
  Respect for the opinions of
    others
  Sense of business etiquette
  Sense of social etiquette
  Sincerity
  Straightforwardness
  Team-orientation
  Warmth
  Willingness to share information

Presentation
  Ability to ask the right questions

  Ability to deliver relevant
    information
  Ability to engage the listener
  Acknowledgment of others
  Articulateness
  Attention to detail
  Awareness of clothing and
    grooming
  Awareness of nonverbal messages
  Awareness of personal space
  Awareness of verbal messages
  Coherence
  Confidence
  Level of formality
  Listening ability
  Respect for confidentiality
  Speed of communication
  Voice tone, pitch, and quality
  Writing ability

Open Mindset
  Acceptance
  Adaptability
  Curiosity
  Flexibility
  Humility
  Interest in learning from others
  Openness to change
  Openness to feedback
  Openness to learning
  Tolerance

In Chapter 3, you will begin to select the list of essential traits for success in the position you want to fill. In deciding the most desirable fundamental traits, you will need to consider the culture, values, and objectives of your organization. Suppose, for example, that work ethic and friendliness are both essential parts of your corporate culture. They would likely appear in a comprehensive list of desirable fundamental traits for any position you seek to fill.

While fundamental traits are not role specific, their relative importance can certainly vary depending on the nature and level of the role. For example, while you may consider work ethic and friendliness as necessary fundamental traits for both a receptionist and a Chief Financial Officer (CFO) in your organization, you may decide that the relative importance of these two traits is different for these roles. Because you will be selecting the most important fundamental traits when preparing to screen candidates, it may be that some fundamental traits you choose as critical for one role may be too low in priority to appear in a selective list for another role.

Analyzing Complementary Traits

In the previous section, we listed fundamental traits that we use to screen candidates for compatibility with an organization for jobs at all levels. But many roles, especially at senior levels, require more sophisticated soft skills. We term the more sophisticated underlying traits complementary fit traits, and we use them to screen for compatibility with particular roles, carefully considering both the nature and the level of each role.

In general, the more senior the role, the more complementary traits are required of an individual. Increasingly senior leadership roles, for example, demand increasingly complex interpersonal skills, and successful leaders must demonstrate an extensive variety of complementary traits.

An effective screening process requires careful selection of the complementary traits that are most critical to a particular role at a particular level. Because of the wide variety of roles that exist at various levels, the list of all the possible complementary traits that could be used for screening is vast. The following selective list includes traits that are important in many leadership roles, but a specific leadership role may require traits that don't appear in this list. (This list appears again as Supplement 3 at the end of the book so that you can refer to it easily as you begin the hiring process.)

Complementary Traits List

Ability to ask open-ended
  questions
Ability to cope with high
  pressure
Ability to deal with ambiguity
Ability to delegate
Ability to establish credibility
Ability to motivate others
Ability to think outside the box
Advanced decision-making
  ability
Advanced listening ability
Advanced problem-solving
  ability
Advanced quality focus
Advanced relationship-
  management ability
Assertiveness
Autonomy
Business acumen
Change-catalyst capacity
Charisma
Collaborative approach
Commitment to business ethics
Conflict-management ability
Continuous-improvement
  outlook
Creativity
Customer-service focus
Decisiveness
Diplomacy
Drive for results
Dynamism
Enjoyment of challenge

Entrepreneurial outlook
Facilitation ability
Forward-thinking ability
Independence
Influencing ability
Initiative
Innovation
Insight
Intellectual capacity
Interpersonal savvy
Intuition
Leadership presence
Managerial courage
Mentoring capacity
Meticulousness
Negotiation ability
Open communication style
Optimism
Perceptiveness
Persuasiveness
Planning ability
Polished presence
Political savvy
Priority-setting ability
Process-improvement
  outlook
Realism
Resourcefulness
Self-development capacity
Stamina
Strategic agility
Vision
Willingness to take calculated
  risks

The complementary traits needed for compatibility with a role vary with both the nature and level of the role. For example, innovation appears in the above list of complementary traits commonly needed for leadership roles. For a clerical support role, innovation may not be one of the key complementary traits needed. Ability to delegate also appears in the list of complementary traits for leadership roles but would likely not appear in the list of complementary traits for a nonsupervisory position. Most roles require some degree of relationship-management ability, but the preceding list for leadership roles includes advanced relationship-management ability as a more likely requirement for success at this level.

Promoting or moving an individual laterally within an organization can be a very positive step in retaining great staff. But different roles typically require different sets of skills. An individual who fits the soft-skill requirements of one role doesn't necessarily have all the soft skills required for another role, even in the same organization. Even if the individual has the required soft skills, they may not be developed to the level of sophistication required for success in the new role. The individual may need mentoring support or other professional development to be successful. Or it may be that the individual is simply not suitable for the new role. Organizations always need to map the soft skills needed for a role, whether hiring externally or promoting or transferring from within.

Fit in Action: Focusing on Traits

We conduct searches for a large, highly successful, entrepreneurial company, which is growing through acquisitions. It focuses intently on customer quality and operates with a very flat structure. Leaders and staff need to make decisions quickly. If they need to revise a course of action based on new information or new developments, all individuals must hold themselves accountable for their decisions.

To maintain its high standards, the company can't accommodate a culture of blame. Employees can't hold others responsible for past mistakes. They simply must correct them and move on. The president therefore believes that a leader's success in his company depends heavily on the trait of accountability, which appears in our list of fundamental traits under the category of Productivity.

When I help this company to hire a new employee, accountability is a key trait I screen for to ensure compatibility with the company, especially for leadership roles. I discuss this trait with the hiring manager in my recommendation of each suitable individual for the short list.

CHAPTER 3

Building Your Fit-Trait Lists

In establishing fit, you must determine the key traits required to succeed in both the organization and the specific role. To do this, you need to consider the culture of the organization and the nature and level of the role. You need to identify, for example, the people within and outside the organization who will interact with the individual in the role. The number and nature of these interactions will influence the level of skill required of a candidate in relationship building and will affect your choice of key traits that support relationship building.

When you select key traits, you may feel tempted to look for a candidate with the entire set of fundamental and complementary traits that would support success in the organization and the role. But this approach sets the bar too high for even the most promising candidate, and you will need to refine your choices to a more realistic number. You will have to think deeply about the type of person best suited to the organization and the role and to distinguish between the critical traits and those that are just nice to have.

Being Aware of Traits in Combination

In this book, we've broken down the elements of behavior into individual traits to help you build a picture of a desirable candidate for your organization and for a particular role. One of the more complicated aspects of assessing fit is that most behaviors result from a combination of traits. It's important to stress that any *one personality trait alone doesn't give you an accurate picture of likely behavior*. For instance, suppose you want to find a candidate who can easily build connections with others. There are many traits that can contribute to varying degrees, including the following fundamental traits: listening ability, respect for the opinions of others, self-awareness, empathy, integrity, friendliness, and sincerity.

You need to decide which of these are most important in your context. This choice may be influenced by the fact that the same trait can contribute to more than one behavior. Suppose, for example, that your organization works in a sector such as health care and that compassionate and ethical behaviors are essential requirements. The fundamental traits that contribute to these behaviors include empathy and integrity, which also appear in the foregoing example for easily building connections with others. Therefore, you may decide that, if easily building connections with others and compassionate and ethical behaviors are all essential, then the traits of empathy and integrity should appear in your list of key fundamental traits.

Who Should Build the List of Traits?

Before you begin to screen candidates for a role, it's imperative that all the key stakeholders agree on the traits that the preferred candidate should have. You also need to decide how many interviewers will be included in the hiring process and to ensure that they can commit to the hiring timelines. (In Chapter 9, we will discuss the appropriate number of interviewers for roles at different levels and the optimum scheduling of interviews.) *Everyone involved in interviewing candidates should reach a consensus on the most important traits.* All interviewers need to agree on what they're looking for and approach the interviews accordingly. Otherwise, subsequent discussions to choose the best candidate are likely to be unfocused and to result in decisions made more on the basis of gut feel than on a clearly reasoned examination of fit.

An essential requirement for an informed choice of key traits is a clear understanding of the nature of the organization and the nature of the role. Interviewers should know from their own experience the traits required and valued by the organization as a whole. However, aside from the hiring manager, they're unlikely to know the ins and outs of the specific role. So interviewers should receive an overview of the job description *before* thinking about what traits will be required for the role. In Chapter 4, we will discuss the content of the overview and the transformation of the job description to a complete position profile that incorporates the selected fundamental and complementary traits.

The way in which you organize the choice of traits may vary. Some interviewers may prefer to choose the traits by working collaboratively in a group and exchanging ideas during the trait selection process. In other cases, interviewers may prefer to make their choices independently and then get together to discuss the thinking behind their choices and reach a consensus.

In making your individual or collective choices, you must ensure that you've considered the views of key stakeholders in the organization. The choice of how broad to make the discussion depends on the nature and level of the role to be filled. For a leadership role involving staff supervision, your list of key stakeholders might include the following:

- The individuals who interact most often with the role, including the person to whom the role reports directly and leaders in other functional areas who interact with the role
- Individuals responsible for the long-term success of the company, such as the president and the executive management team, including the individual in charge of human resources
- Peers of the role
- Staff ranked immediately below the role

Selecting Fundamental Traits

You, and the other interviewers, might begin by thinking about the 10 to 15 most critical fundamental traits that an individual needs to succeed in your organization. The list of fundamental traits in Chapter 2 will give you a starting point. Because we find that all five categories of fundamental traits described in Chapter 2 are important, you might try identifying two or three critical fundamental traits from each category. However, such a uniform distribution of fundamental traits between the categories may not always be the most appropriate choice. For instance, suppose you have to fill a role that interacts very little with others. You will almost certainly want an individual with sufficient interpersonal skills to work well with his or her boss, but the emphasis of the role may be more on productivity than on building relationships. In this case, you may want to select more fundamental traits from the Productivity section than from the Relationship-Building section of the list.

If the choice of fundamental traits is to achieve its purpose in screening for the best fit, then honesty about the true nature of the organization is essential. For example, suppose an organization presents itself as highly responsive to changing circumstances, but the reality is a hierarchical setting in which important decisions can be slow in coming. An honest appraisal of the nature of the organization might result in a discussion of such fundamental traits as patience and self-control among possible contributors to long-term success in the organization.

Answering the following questions will help with the final list of choices:

1. Which behaviors are essential for success in the culture of the organization and are expected of every employee?
2. What are the most important fundamental traits that contribute to each essential behavior?
3. Are there any fundamental traits that appear repeatedly in the answer to question 2?
4. Of individuals who have succeeded with your organization in the past, what fundamental traits have contributed most to their success?
5. Of individuals who have not been a good fit with your organization, what fundamental traits did they lack?
6. Does the current condition of your organization affect your list of fundamental traits required for fit? For example, is the organization growing, undergoing rapid change, or downsizing? If so, are there additional fundamental traits that this changing environment requires for success?
7. Is your organization culturally diverse or becoming more so? Is there any impact on the fundamental traits required for fit?
8. Have you reached a final agreement on which members of your organization will be involved in interviewing candidates?
9. Have all interviewers been asked to choose the most important fundamental traits?
10. Have all interviewers reached a consensus on the most important fundamental traits?

Fundamental Traits Rating Table

When you've agreed on the key fundamental traits, record them in the appropriate categories of Table 3.1. (This table also appears as Supplement 4 at the end of this book.) After you interview the short-listed candidates, you will use this table to rate each candidate on each selected fundamental trait.

Table 3.1 Recording and rating fundamental traits

	Strong									Weak
Productivity	10	9	8	7	6	5	4	3	2	1
Trait										
Trait										
Trait										

	Strong									Weak
Self-management	10	9	8	7	6	5	4	3	2	1
Trait										
Trait										
Trait										

	Strong									Weak
Relationship building	10	9	8	7	6	5	4	3	2	1
Trait										
Trait										
Trait										

	Strong									Weak
Presentation	10	9	8	7	6	5	4	3	2	1
Trait										
Trait										
Trait										

	Strong									Weak
Open mindset	10	9	8	7	6	5	4	3	2	1
Trait										
Trait										
Trait										

Selecting Complementary Traits

We find that the optimum number of complementary traits identified as critical for a role depends on the seniority of the role. In Table 3.2, we suggest approximate guidelines.

Table 3.2 *Complementary traits and role level*

Level of role	Appropriate number of complementary traits
Nonsupervisory	5
Managerial	5–8
Director	8–10
C-level	10–15

The list of complementary traits in Chapter 2 will give you a starting point for your selection, but keep in mind that key complementary traits vary widely with the nature and level of a role. Don't be limited by the list in Chapter 2 if you're hiring for a role demanding other complementary traits. Answering the following questions will help with your choices:

1. Which behaviors are essential for success in meeting the demands of the specific role?
2. What are the most important complementary traits that contribute to each of these essential behaviors?
3. Are there any complementary traits that appear repeatedly in the answer to question 2?
4. Which complementary traits does a candidate need from day one with your organization, and which complementary traits might the candidate develop in the role?
5. Of individuals who have succeeded in this role or a similar role in your organization in the past, what complementary traits have contributed most to their success?
6. Of individuals who have not been a good fit with this role or a similar role in your organization, what complementary traits did they lack?
7. Do expected changes in the role affect your list of complementary traits required for fit? Is the role expanding or undergoing rapid changes? Are there additional complementary traits that will be required as the role unfolds?

8. If you expect the candidate to advance through the organization, do your expectations influence your selection of priority complementary traits? What additional complementary traits will the candidate require for a promotion?

9. Who will interact with the new employee? What complementary traits will the individual need in order to establish and maintain great relationships with these specific individuals, including the direct boss?

10. Have all interviewers been asked to choose the most important complementary traits?

11. Have all interviewers reached a consensus on the most important complementary traits?

Answering the second part of question 9 can be challenging. New hires have to deal with the personalities around them, especially that of the person they report to. Part of defining the necessary qualities of a new hire is to examine the personality match with the direct boss. For a boss to express accurately what they're like to work with requires a high level of self-awareness, honesty, and, sometimes, political courage.

It's often difficult for a boss to step back and examine the traits that they will bring to the new relationship. This examination includes answering such questions as "What traits will the new hire need in order to deal with my management style and personality quirks?" An objective outside assessment is often required to consider what traits of the boss and a potential new hire would be compatible and what traits would be an annoyance to either party, possibly decreasing effectiveness or producing conflict. One of the key roles of a search firm is to look at this delicate match between boss and direct report when undertaking a search.

Complementary Traits Rating Table

When you've agreed on the key complementary traits, record them in Table 3.3. (This table also appears as Supplement 5 at the end of this book.)

Table 3.3 Recording and rating complementary traits

	Strong									Weak
	10	9	8	7	6	5	4	3	2	1
Trait										
Trait										
Trait										
Trait										
Trait										
Trait										
Trait										
Trait										
Trait										
Trait										
Trait										
Trait										
Trait										
Trait										
Trait										

At this stage, all interviewers should have the same fundamental and complementary traits listed in Tables 3.1 and 3.3. These tables will next be used to record assessments of candidates during the screening process. You may find it helpful to track completion of the steps in the TAP using the Hiring-for-Fit Checklist in Supplement 1 at the end of this book. You've now completed the first four steps in the checklist.

Fit in Action: Picking the Right Traits

The CFO of a small, sophisticated head office wanted to add to his Finance Department and create a team of individuals who could work closely together, even though most staff members in the department were specialists who had become accustomed to working independently. The CFO asked us to help in finding technically skilled individuals who also had the interpersonal skills to forge relationships with others on the team.

Before we began the search, we worked with the CFO and the other interviewers to identify 15 key fundamental traits and 8 key complementary traits that would be required of new hires to help build a more unified department. The most critical fundamental trait was a willingness to share information, and the most critical complementary trait was a collaborative approach.

Referring to the agreed lists as they interviewed candidates, the interviewers could focus on the specific traits required for success in unifying the department. Instead of overconcentrating on hard skills, the CFO could now select candidates who best demonstrated the interpersonal skills that the company needed for its long-term success. As a result, the company improved its track record in hiring and retaining individuals with the right fit.

CHAPTER 4

From Job Description to Position Profile

We find that few organizations have a clear and accurate job description at the outset of a search. Perhaps surprisingly, we see many managers hiring new employees using out-of-date job descriptions, even after an organization has changed considerably since it last hired. A document often exists, but in many cases it fails to capture important elements of the organization and the role. In particular, we see many job descriptions that emphasize hard-skill requirements and pay little, if any, attention to soft skills. This is a serious oversight, given that the dismissal of employees usually results from deficiencies in soft skills, not hard skills.

The process of choosing the necessary fundamental and complementary traits for the role, described in Chapter 3, often involves intense discussions of the nature and scope of the role and the ways in which it might evolve over time. Reaching a well-founded consensus over the necessary traits inevitably requires agreement on the present and future responsibilities of the role. Therefore, a detailed and accurate job description is an essential starting point. However, we find that a traditional job description, with its focus on *what* needs to be done, falls short when it comes to hiring for fit.

In our executive search practice, we've greatly enhanced the job description as a tool in hiring for fit. We term the enhanced version a **position profile**, which describes not only *what* needs to be done but *how* it needs to be done. A well-crafted position profile has many advantages, which we will describe later in this chapter.

Starting with an Overview

In order to be able to make informed choices about essential traits, interviewers need an overview of the role *before* the group discussion of which fit traits the role requires. The hiring manager typically produces an initial draft of the overview, which outlines:

1. The overall mandate of the role and the expected outcomes
2. The history of the role, including whether it's a new role or a replacement hire into an existing role
3. The key responsibilities and the time allotted to key areas
4. The key deliverables, including what needs to be achieved and when
5. The positioning of the role in the organizational chart
   - Who does the role report to?
   - How many staff report to the role?
   - What level of person does the role interact with?
   - What departments does the role interact with cross-functionally?
   - Who does it interact with externally?
6. How the role is expected to evolve over time
7. The projected career path of the person in the role

This information sets the stage for discussions of both the fundamental and complementary fit traits required, as described in Chapter 3. (As noted in Chapter 2, fundamental traits are not role specific, but their relative importance can vary with the nature and level of the role.)

After interviewers have agreed on the essential traits, the overview can be transformed into a position profile. The process of writing a position profile can be time consuming. Because we're convinced of the value of the position profile in hiring for fit and supporting a smooth transition, we highly recommend its use in your search process. We suggest that you incorporate the following enhancements:

- Linking the required traits to the key responsibilities of the role
- Establishing the level of responsibility for each aspect of the role
- Clarifying relationship-management requirements by indicating individuals the new hire will interact with on different tasks, what they will do together, and the nature of the relationship required
- Specifying required achievement levels in specific responsibilities and in high-priority objectives

The next four sections include examples that show how we create a position profile from an overview after the interviewers agree on the essential traits for the role. Because the final position profile is so much more comprehensive than the overview on which it's based, we sometimes find that the client's review of the position profile, and subsequent discussions with us, lead to refinement of the lists of essential traits. Refining these lists is a positive development, as long as interviewers complete and agree upon the lists before the prescreening and interviews begin.

Incorporating Traits

Incorporating the necessary traits means much more than listing them at the end of a traditional job description or in the Qualifications section of a job posting. The more sophisticated position profile incorporates the required fundamental and complementary traits into the responsibilities of the role and links these traits to behaviors required by the organization and to job-specific activities. Boldfaced words in the following examples specify required traits in position profiles, either literally or through the use of a closely related term.

> **Job description**: Manages the Operations Department
>
> **Position profile**: Makes **timeliness** the cornerstone of the Operations Department, **prioritizes** tasks accordingly, and **clearly communicates** monthly progress to senior management

A particular statement in a position profile may contain a mix of fundamental and complementary traits as in the preceding example. Other statements may include only one or the other:

- Pitches in to support the work of colleagues and contributes to the **positive, respectful**, and **team-oriented** atmosphere in the company (This statement reflects a general requirement of all employees in an organization and contains only fundamental traits.)
- Contributes to decisions that affect the **strategic direction** of the company by applying **business acumen** and an **ability to drive change** (This statement contains only complementary traits in a senior leadership responsibility.)

Portraying Responsibility Level

A thorough position profile sets expectations regarding the level of responsibility of the work to be done. Incorporating these expectations requires answers to such questions as the following:

- Does the entire responsibility for a task lie with this role, or does the individual assist someone more senior?
- Does the task require delegation? If so, what level of leadership or management does it demand?
- Is this a hands-on task or more of a facilitation task?
- Does the task require the individual to initiate an action?
- Is this a new task requiring the individual to develop an approach or create a solution?

The boldfaced parts of the following examples show how the position profile can more clearly establish responsibility and accountability.

- **Takes full responsibility for** the timeliness and accuracy of the annual budget
- **Advises** and **supports** the VP of Sales in the development of a long-term sales strategy by sharing in-depth operational knowledge

The position profile can indicate how the expectations of a role are expected to evolve. The following example includes the expression "increasingly over time" to suggest that the role will place an increased emphasis on planning ability in the future.

- **Works collaboratively with** the management team and **increasingly over time contributes to the operational plan**

Clarifying Relationship-Management Requirements

The position profile should also clarify who else in the organization is involved in the task and the nature of their involvement. It should answer such questions as the following:

- Is this a task to be undertaken independently? If not, who else is involved?
- What is the level of input from others?

- Is the task designed to support someone else? If so, in what way?
- What relationships must develop for effective completion of the task?

The boldfaced parts of the following examples show relationship-management requirements.

- Makes **joint presentations with one of the partners** at **client meetings** to reinforce the company's commitment to client service and to bid more effectively for new business
- Works **with colleagues in the Sales Department as a team** to examine any overlapping contacts and **discuss and agree on a fair approach** to leveraging all connections most productively

Incorporating Required Achievements

The position profile can set clear accountability parameters for the role by including information about the achievement expectations for specific responsibilities.

- Delegates authority along with accountability and **holds department managers and supervisors accountable for meeting their functional responsibilities, goals, and objectives and maintaining a high level of performance**
- Plans and coordinates the year-end audit and liaises with external auditors, providing thorough, accurate information **to ensure a clean audit**

Here are other examples of responsibilities that incorporate required achievements:

- Communicates information openly and inclusively across the organization **to promote positive relationships, efficient problem-solving, and high productivity**
- Implements and continuously improves a comprehensive Health and Safety Program that maintains enforcement of rules and procedures **to reduce the frequency of workplace accidents**

In the position profile, we stress particularly important required achievements by including sections on *key 6-month and 1-year objectives* after the list of specific responsibilities. Each objective is based on one or more of the specific responsibilities, for example:

- Works closely with IT to implement a new Enterprise Resource Planning (ERP) system **in a timely and cost-effective manner**, obtaining ongoing feedback from all system users **to identify and address training needs and optimize accuracy and efficiency**

Seven Advantages of a Position Profile

A position profile has considerable advantages over a traditional job description, including the following:

1. Clearly describing the behaviors that the organization and the role require, based on the necessary hard and soft skills
2. Acting as an ongoing reference for interviewers at various stages of the screening process and providing a detailed understanding of your requirements to outside recruiters, if you're using them to identify a short list
3. Providing a solid basis for future performance reviews in the areas of both hard and soft skills by including both in the responsibilities of the role and by specifying required achievement levels
4. Indicating how the position is expected to evolve over time and specifying additional hard and soft skills that will be needed in the future
5. Providing a powerful marketing tool for attracting the best candidates to your organization, since the thoroughness and clarity of the document stand out among the typical, quite sketchy, job descriptions that candidates often see
6. Painting your organization and the quality of its management in a very positive light, and so contributing to the "word on the street" about your organization as an employer of choice
7. Being of tremendous help to a new hire in understanding the expectations of the role, particularly with respect to working with others

Relying on an incomplete or out-of-date job description in the hiring process increases the risk of hiring the wrong person. That may seem overly alarmist, but I've seen thousands of job descriptions and can attest to that fact. I can tell you without reservation that, with an out-of-date or poorly written job description, an organization will likely hire a candidate who doesn't have all the necessary soft-skill traits for the role. To put it another way, if an organization doesn't have sufficient information to produce an accurate, detailed, and up-to-date job description, there's been insufficient discussion of the role and the qualities of the person needed to fill it. Achieving a good fit in these circumstances is a very iffy proposition.

As a critical part of an executive search, we gather a great deal of information from the client about both the hard-skill requirements and the essential soft-skill traits. Using this information to rewrite the client's job description into a position profile, to incorporate both the hard and soft skills required, is essential preparation for screening candidates more precisely and selecting individuals who can do the job, grow in the role, and advance with the organization.

Fit in Action: Attracting Strong Candidates

We conducted a search for a senior leader whose role required a particularly complex set of hard and soft skills. Because of the organization's location, and its wish to hire a local candidate, we had a limited pool of candidates to recruit from. To make sure that we attracted the best ones, we spent a considerable amount of time preparing a detailed position profile that accurately captured the critical details of the organization and the role, including both the hard-skill and soft-skill requirements for success.

One of the short-listed candidates said that the position profile, which she received after our initial screening meeting, had convinced her to pursue the position because it indicated to her that the company had high standards and a clear focus. The position profile had impressed her not only by emphasizing the required outcomes of the role, but also by articulating clearly the behaviors required to build successful relationships with others in the company. The position profile also clearly indicated ways in which the role was expected to develop over time, laying a foundation for future advancement within the company. This forward-looking aspect of the position profile reassured the candidate that the company paid attention to the long-term well-being of its employees.

CHAPTER 5

The Importance of Candidate Expectations

Unless you know exactly which hard and soft skills a role requires for success, you can't screen candidates effectively for the right fit. However, while you need to ensure that the candidate meets the expectations of the organization and the role, you also need to consider another essential component of fit by ensuring the compatibility of the organization and the role with the candidate's expectations. To examine fit with the candidate's expectations, *you need to assess the reasons why the candidate wants the job.* There are many aspects to explore, including the following:

- Checking the candidate's motivation to make a move at this time
- Assessing the alignment of the organization's expectations with the candidate's expectations about a future career path, including growth or advancement
- Assessing the alignment of the role with the candidate's immediate and future compensation expectations
- Ensuring that the location and work demands meets the candidate's individual and family expectations

Eleven Drivers of Candidate Motivation

Why does the candidate really want a new job? By checking the motives behind a candidate's decision to change jobs, you can gain useful insight into the fit of the organization and the role with the individual's expectations. These motives may include:

1. Ambition for promotion earlier than the candidate's current job allows
2. Limited future opportunities for professional development with the current employer

3. A wish for a more interesting or challenging role
4. A wish for a better-paying job
5. Inadequate performance and a desire to move from the current job before being let go
6. Uncertainty about the future because of corporate restructuring
7. A desire for a new job after termination from the previous role
8. Interpersonal conflict with a current boss
9. A desire to work in a location closer to home to reduce commuting time
10. A desire to improve work–life balance and reduce hours spent working
11. A desire for flexibility at work to accommodate personal or family needs or preferences

It may be that a candidate, for personal or family reasons, wants to work only 35 hours per week. But if the organization wants the new hire to progress into increasingly senior management positions, the fit will most probably not be right. Even with all the right hard and soft skills for the initial role, the candidate is unlikely to be a good fit for the organization over the longer term.

Assessing Career Path Compatibility

One common pitfall in emphasizing hard skills over soft skills arises when hiring a candidate who has held essentially the same role in another organization. On the surface, the candidate may seem very appealing because there's a very close match between the hard skills required by the two roles. But an individual who moves from another organization into the same job in your organization may be bored by the work and see no challenge ahead after adjusting to the new environment. The new hire may expect a promotion in a shorter period than your organization can provide and may feel restless in the meantime. If the promise of advancement feels too slow in coming, the new employee may soon start looking elsewhere for opportunities or be open to approaches from headhunters.

To avoid losing new hires, it's especially important to ensure compatibility of the candidate's and your organization's expectations in this situation. You need to be clear on the following:

- Do you need to hire a candidate who seeks career growth and promotions? If you do, what are the opportunities in your organization for learning new skills and acquiring and refining advanced capabilities as the role unfolds? How quickly will the individual be promoted within your organization? Are these realities compatible with the expectations of specific candidates?
- Do you need to hire a candidate who will happily do the same role over the long term? If you do, is there a candidate who wants this situation? If so, what is the individual's motivation for continuing to perform well in the role over time? Does the individual's outlook align with the company's expectations for performance in the role?

Assessing Compensation Compatibility

In our career coaching practice, we hear of many hiring processes in which there is no discussion of compensation with candidates until an offer is made and turned down. To ensure that there are no unwelcome surprises at the offer stage with the final candidate, you need to set a salary range before the search begins. You also need to consider other aspects of compensation, when applicable, such as a bonus or a company car. It's prudent to have an initial conversation with potential candidates about their ballpark compensation expectations very early in the screening process, or you may find yourself in the position of interviewing candidates you won't be able to attract.

Your compensation range largely determines the level and caliber of individual you can hire. To select the right range, you need to be informed about the current market to know whether a particular range will attract the candidate you want to hire. You may obtain this information by engaging a knowledgeable search firm or by networking within your industry. The information you obtain will guide you on the level and caliber of applicant that particular ranges can attract.

Challenges in setting a suitable compensation range can arise when you try to maintain consistency with your organization's existing compensation structure. Rather than conducting a search with low compensation and failing to attract the caliber or level of candidate you require, you may need to reconsider the parameters of the role and your list of essential hard and soft skills.

Many hiring managers ignore the conversation with candidates about compensation because they don't know how to approach it. They wait until the end of the hiring process and hope for the best. However, an early discussion on the subject projects transparency and eases the way for future discussions. Since you can't start negotiating salary until both sides have full knowledge of each other, it's best to ask candidates for only broad compensation expectations at an early screening stage. If their expected compensation range is in line with what you can offer, then this is a basis for continued conversation.

Midway through the process, another conversation with the remaining candidates about compensation will allow you to check whether their expectations have changed and to ensure that their compensation expectations are still compatible with your range. Candidates' expectations can certainly change, depending on a variety of factors, such as their level of interest in the position, other opportunities they have in the works, changes occurring to their current role or employer, or changes in market conditions.

Your aim when you reach the offer stage is to present an offer that's fair and acceptable to both sides so that your preferred candidate accepts the position. A transparent approach to compensation and a fair offer will create goodwill right from the start of the hire and will set the tone for a successful transition.

Assessing Location and Work-Demands Compatibility

It may seem obvious that the location of the job needs to work for a potential candidate, but we've seen many candidates accept positions that have long commutes. In some cases, they accepted because they'd been unemployed for a long period. Other candidates accepted attractive offers without thinking through the implications for their families. And before too long, many of the individuals with long commutes elected to leave the organizations they'd recently joined. But in other cases, individuals have had no problem commuting great distances over the long term for a dream job. So it's important that you understand the real motivation of the candidate you're considering.

Equally important, you need to assess a candidate's openness and willingness to travel, if this is part of the role or if you expect the candidate to advance to a future role that requires travel.

You also need to ensure compatibility of a candidate's expectations with the work demands of the role. With technology allowing employees to be on call around the clock, together with the demands of a global workplace, the conversation may need to cover not only the number of hours to be worked but also the flexibility to work at unusual times. Many roles include deadline-driven responsibilities, such as major reports, year-end accounting, or time-sensitive troubleshooting, and so work demands can increase significantly at certain times. In such cases, you need to check that the candidate is willing and able to accommodate the pressure points as well as the regular day-to-day responsibilities.

In the first five chapters of this book, we've looked at the elements of fit from both the employer's perspective and the candidate's perspective. The next step in our comprehensive TAP is to understand how to screen candidates effectively for the best fit. The next chapter discusses an often-overlooked opportunity to reduce the time the screening process takes.

Fit in Action: Staying Alert for Changes in Motivation

We recently identified a candidate who seemed like a great fit for a role in a client's organization. She had all the required traits. The role involved extensive client service, and so the successful candidate needed to demonstrate the trait of responsiveness. This candidate had clearly demonstrated responsiveness in the early screening stages. She'd responded in a timely manner to our e-mails and provided all the information we'd requested before and during our interview with her.

After her first interview with the client, her behavior changed. She stopped responding promptly to our calls and e-mails. Despite our initial positive impressions, we told the client that we now had concerns about the candidate's level of responsiveness. As a result, the client moved forward with another candidate on the short list.

We followed up with the initially promising candidate to let her know that the client didn't intend to call her back for a second interview. At that point, she told us that, the day after her first interview, she'd received an offer from another organization that seemed more appealing. She now felt less motivation to pursue our client's job.

We first screen for motivation in the initial stages of the search before selecting the short list. Although individuals on the short list might meet all of your requirements for fit, their circumstances can change during the process. As our client learned from its experience with the initially promising candidate, such screening must continue through the entire process of hiring.

CHAPTER 6

Prescreening for Fit

We refer to the screening that takes place before an interview as **prescreening**. Most organizations use prescreening to screen primarily for hard skills, but this emphasis misses a great opportunity to screen for the broader aspects of fit. A significant part of the screening for soft-skill fit and compatibility of expectations can and should occur at the prescreening stage, before you make a decision on granting a first interview. We consider prescreening a valuable tool in arriving at a strong short list of candidates who might fit the organization and the role, subject to more in-depth investigation. If a search firm isn't involved in hiring for the role, prescreening can typically be completed by the HR Department or the hiring manager.

Prescreening to eliminate candidates on the basis of their hard and soft skills or incompatible expectations has become more important with the growing power of electronic media. Resumes and cover letters can now be quickly submitted to multiple organizations with ease, leading many applicants to avoid taking the time to customize their application for a particular role or a particular organization. In our search practice, we receive many applications from individuals who clearly haven't carefully read the information in the posting. And often, they have little motivation in pursuing this particular opportunity but have submitted their résumé to make a general contact for other opportunities. A failure to eliminate these individuals from contention early in the process can cost a great deal of time and wasted effort later.

As described in previous chapters, the hiring process begins with defining your key hiring traits for the organization and the role and developing an awareness of any limitations your organization might have in meeting candidate expectations. Once you've compiled your list of key traits, everyone involved in the search can use it to assess the behaviors of potential candidates as early as their initial contact, including their application letters and resumes, any notes or other written material, and any telephone contact. In some cases, you may know, or know of, a candidate and be in an even better position to prescreen for soft-skill fit and compatibility of expectations before deciding on an interview.

It's important to keep in mind that actions speak louder than words. *What people do reveals far more about them than what they say.* By observing behaviors, you can infer underlying traits. Through careful observation of a number of behaviors, you can build a fuller picture of many of the candidate's traits and also identify areas of concern that require further investigation in any subsequent interview.

Initial Application Prescreening

Eliminating candidates on the basis of carelessness, such as typographical errors or unclear wording in resumes and cover letters, is a common feature of traditional prescreening. But trait-based prescreening can go much further and can allow you to focus on the traits already identified as critical to the organization and the role. For example, if the candidate submits a generic application letter, not customized to the specific role, what questions does this raise about the candidate's motivation and some of the candidate's traits, such as will to succeed, work ethic, and adaptability? Are any of these traits essential to the organization or the role?

This one behavior may not give enough evidence to result in a decision on whether the candidate should advance, but it contributes to a picture of the candidate's traits. As you experience other behaviors, you can look for consistency in their implications about underlying traits. Areas of inconsistency can prompt further investigation, either during prescreening or, if appropriate, in interviews.

In job advertisements we place for leadership roles, we ask candidates to include with their applications a cover letter that addresses important aspects of the soft skills required to succeed in the role and the organization. We might ask candidates to give examples to describe how their ability to build relationships across an organization has contributed to its success; how their attitude to their work affects the people around them; or how their openness to feedback has contributed to their professional development. Candidates are clearly free to craft responses that place them in a flattering light, so the content of the responses may give little direct insight. However, other behaviors can speak volumes about a candidate.

Perhaps the most surprising behavior we observe from the majority of candidates, sometimes up to 80 percent or more for a particular role, is a complete failure to provide the requested information. This behavior raises serious questions about some fundamental traits, including responsiveness, industriousness, cooperativeness, and follow-through, as well as about the level of motivation in applying for the role. The minority of candidates who do comply immediately set themselves apart. Requiring specific tasks as part of the application process can hence act as a powerful filter.

Many candidates submit professionally written resumes these days, so the additional writing task—likely completed in a much shorter time—may expose shortcomings that the quality of the résumé may mask. You can ask yourself what the quality of the response to the writing task indicates about such fundamental traits as organizational ability, attention to detail, commitment to quality, and coherence. Are the candidate's written communication skills up to the demands of the role? Is the evidence about communication skills the same from the résumé and the additional writing task?

E-mail Prescreening

After using the initial application as a first filter, you can continue prescreening for fit by contacting everyone on your long list by e-mail to ask two or three simple questions. There are many examples of questions you might choose from, including: Why are you interested in this role? What would set you apart from others for this role? What is your intended career path? What role are you ideally looking for? What salary range is acceptable to you?

The wording of the responses sometimes gives useful information about traits. For example, if a candidate is asked what sets him or her apart for a role, does the person demonstrate a balanced view of strengths and accomplishments, or do the responses indicate boastfulness, arrogance, or the attitude of a know-it-all? The wording of the responses often gives useful information about expectations. Some candidates are surprisingly frank, such as the individual who described his goal of opening his own business. This long-term expectation was not compatible with the hiring organization's expectation of a long-term relationship in which the employee would grow in the role and advance to more senior positions.

As with the initial application, much more can be learned from the nature of the response. You might ask yourself:

- Is the response thoughtful and well organized or shallow and carelessly constructed?
- Has the individual invested time and energy into responding, or was the response dashed off?
- Is the tone professional and respectful, and does it demonstrate an awareness of who the reader is?
- Was the response timely? If it wasn't, did the candidate make the effort to provide a plausible explanation?
- What is the candidate's level of ability to communicate?
- Do the traits and level of motivation that you might infer from the observed behaviors strengthen or weaken impressions you gained from the initial application?
- Is a picture of the candidate beginning to emerge with respect to any of the critical fit traits for the role?

LinkedIn and Other Online Prescreening

Many professionals maintain an online business presence, such as a LinkedIn profile. Although many LinkedIn profiles have little detail, they often provide a quick snapshot of career progression and contain enough information to contribute to your assessment of candidates' traits. You can also refer to other social media sites, including Facebook, but LinkedIn and other business-oriented sites usually provide the most instructive information.

There are many aspects of a LinkedIn or other online profile you might consider, including the following:

- What does the photograph reveal about the candidate? What can you infer from the facial pose? If the photograph isn't limited to the face, what does the body language reveal? Can you infer anything about such traits as confidence or positive attitude?

- What does the written content say about the candidate? What information has the candidate chosen to accentuate? Does the writing show good organization, clarity, and attention to detail?

- Does the information in the profile agree with the candidate's résumé, or are there contradictions in dates, credentials, or other content? Are there possible questions about the candidate's attention to detail or honesty?

- How successfully has the candidate progressed along his or her career path? How quickly has the candidate advanced? Does the candidate's rate of progression correspond with your organization's expectations for the role that it needs to fill?

- How does the LinkedIn and other online prescreening add to the emerging picture of the candidate's traits and expectations?

Phone Prescreening

After initial assessment of the application, traditional prescreening often continues with a short telephone conversation to assess a candidate's hard skills, salary expectations, and location requirements. This conversation thus provides insight into the candidate's expectations, as well as job-specific skills and experience. However, this conversation can be used to illuminate many of the candidate's traits as well. For example:

- Before you speak to the person, listen to his or her voice-mail greeting. Does it reveal such traits as positive attitude, energy level, confidence, or sense of social etiquette?

- What does the voice-mail greeting indicate about verbal communication ability?

- How easy or hard has the candidate made the scheduling of the call? Has the candidate been respectful of your time? Is the individual on time for the call? Can you draw conclusions about such traits as cooperativeness, dependability, punctuality, or sense of business etiquette?

- When you speak to the candidate, are his or her conversational skills consistent in sophistication and tone with the recorded greeting? Are the candidate's answers to questions coherent and clearly expressed, or are they rambling and confused?

- Has the candidate prepared for your scheduled call? Is the candidate familiar with the job posting? Does the candidate have a résumé at hand in readiness to address any questions you have about it? What might you conclude about such traits as diligence and dependability? What can you tell about the candidate's motivation?

- Does the individual respond to your questions by openly and willingly sharing information or with evasive answers? Can you infer anything about the candidate's responsiveness, cooperativeness, reasonableness, or honesty?

- Does the candidate make an effort to connect with you? Is the candidate friendly and polite?

- How well does the candidate listen when you ask questions?

- Does the candidate know how to inject suitable humor into a conversation? Does the candidate lack humor altogether? Are any attempts at humor inappropriate or offensive? Can you learn anything about such traits as self-awareness, judgment, or tolerance from the candidate's use of humor?

- When given the opportunity to ask questions, does the candidate seem interested in finding out more about the organization and the role?

From everything that you now know about the candidate's traits and expectations, is it possible that the candidate might be a good fit for the organization and the role? If not, there's no need to interview this candidate.

Fit in Action: Observing Behaviors in Prescreening

For a search that included an investor relations component, our client required us to search for candidates with particularly strong communication skills, including sophisticated writing ability. The role also required the complementary traits of advanced relationship-management ability and influencing ability, and high degrees of interpersonal and political savvy, in order to deal effectively with a diverse group of individuals who could be demanding.

One of the long-listed candidates looked very promising. His résumé revealed that he'd tracked very quickly, and his submission suggested very strong written skills. However, when we conducted our phone prescreening of this candidate, we were surprised at what we encountered.

In scheduling the phone conversation by e-mail, we found that the tone of the candidate's responses was overly familiar, as if he was writing to a close friend rather than a new business contact. This tone was troubling to us since the role required a very strong need to understand your audience and to select your wording and approach carefully. In the phone conversation itself, the individual was, for the most part, open, enthusiastic, and easy to talk to. However, when asked questions that he didn't know how to answer, he sounded a little aggressive and refused to respond.

Since our client was looking for a person who would be able to handle tough questions and delicate situations, the candidate's responses indicated a lack of ability or experience in these areas, and perhaps signaled a lack of maturity. Consequently, we didn't select him for our short list and we moved forward with other candidates who were a closer fit to the client's needs.

CHAPTER 7

Approaching Interviews with Fit in Mind

With your expectations clearly defined, your agreed-upon lists of key fundamental and complementary traits, and the completion of prescreening (either by your organization or a search firm), you're ready to begin interviewing short-listed candidates. Having done the groundwork required in hiring for fit, it's important not to fall back into familiar ways of interviewing, which rely too heavily on gut instinct and not sufficiently on a more thorough exploration of traits. It's important to maintain your focus on fit throughout the interviewing stages, and it helps if you keep some important aspects in mind.

Taking Gut Instinct to the Next Level

Instinct plays an important role in assessing a candidate, but there are dangers in relying on it without further analysis. I've often heard a hiring manager sum up an assessment of a candidate by saying, simply, "I like him." But that doesn't reveal enough information. To make a well-founded decision to hire the candidate, you have to understand more specifically why you feel this way. Can you identify the traits that make the candidate a good fit with the organization and the role?

If you've articulated clearly the key hiring traits you want to see in a candidate, then your search won't end when you can say "I like him," but when you can say "I like him because he's demonstrated the key traits that we identified when we started our search." By asking questions based on these traits during your interview, you will gain a clear understanding of a candidate's soft-skill fit. Without ignoring your gut instinct, you can now make a much more comprehensive assessment than you could by relying on instinct alone. In addition, the focus on key traits will permit you to discuss your enthusiasm for, or concerns and reservations about, a candidate more analytically and objectively with other interviewers in order to reach a consensus.

That Niggling Feeling

Sometimes you interview a candidate who just doesn't feel right for the job. You should pay attention to that niggling feeling, which can arise in a number of ways. For example, your feeling may arise from discomfort with the candidate's body language or telephone manner or from your reflection on a written comment the candidate provided during prescreening.

That niggling feeling may provide clues about issues you have with the personality of the candidate. But you can't simply rely on the feeling alone. You have to assess it in a way that you can articulate, transforming it from a subconscious sensation into a reasoned thought about the candidate's traits. Think about what traits might underlie the candidate's behavior(s) that triggered your feeling. You can then examine all of the other evidence available to you to see if it reinforces or allays your concerns. By identifying the specific reason that causes you to feel uncertain, you can increase the amount of useful information available for making a hiring decision based on fit.

Be Curious, Not Suspicious

In an interview, a candidate's body language may indicate that he or she isn't giving you the full story. Suppose the candidate shows uncomfortable or exaggerated body language while presenting information, such as shifting his or her eyes from side to side when describing salary expectations. Or perhaps the applicant has facial expressions that don't match the narrative, such as frowning throughout the description of a significant professional achievement. In such situations, get curious.

If you see the candidate's eyes shifting during a description of salary expectations, your first reaction may be unease. But remember that the point of the interview is to clarify the candidate's traits and expectations.

You will never understand the candidate's behavior, or your own unease, unless you ask questions. Perhaps the candidate simply feels nervous in interview situations and will relax as the interaction proceeds. Perhaps the candidate feels awkward or embarrassed while asking for a salary that far exceeds the salary of his previous job. You can probe to find out.

"OK," you may say, "we're considering candidates with a broad range of salary expectations, so I'm interested to know how you arrived at that figure." By explaining why you're asking for this information and making it clear that there's no "right answer," you will sound curious, not hostile. *Curiosity promotes further discussion and enables you to gain further insight into the candidate.* A relaxed discussion encourages the candidate to be more authentic and to exhibit behaviors that are more genuine. A more confrontational approach makes candidates defensive and reduces the amount of information they're willing to share with you. In Chapter 9, we will expand on the misuse of antagonistic questions.

If the candidate frowns while describing a significant achievement, you might follow up with questions that show interest, such as: "That sounds like a lot of work. How heavy was your work load at that time?" or "Looking back, how do you feel about that task?" Again, the aim is to open up the discussion. Don't leave your initial unease unexplored so that unaddressed doubts about the candidate remain. And always stay focused on gaining insight into the candidate's traits and expectations.

By acknowledging and listening to your initial instinct about a candidate, you can take steps to analyze it more deeply and gather more information. You can then determine whether your feeling is based on an assumption or a personal bias or whether it reflects the absence of a key hiring trait in the candidate.

Trait Showstoppers

As noted in Chapter 3, most behaviors result from a combination of traits, and any one personality trait alone doesn't give you an accurate picture of likely behaviors. Having said this, we recognize there are situations in which you may feel that certain individual traits are utterly essential and that their absence makes it impossible to hire the candidate. We call such traits **showstoppers**.

One possible example of a showstopper is the trait of honesty. Perhaps the financial responsibilities of a particular role are such that, to avoid the risk of fraud, any level of dishonesty rules out a candidate. But what if the candidate withholds information in the interview? Do you consider this a lack of honesty, or do you decide to dig for more information? You will need to decide what, if any, traits are showstoppers for the organization and the role and to consider what evidence is sufficient to eliminate candidates on this basis.

Which Traits Must You Hire and Which Traits Can You Coach?

While you may wish to hire an individual who is "perfect" in every way, the reality is that, no matter how carefully you screen, *the hiring process inevitably requires some trade-offs*. What can you live with, and what can you not? Suppose a candidate isn't as strong as you would like in an important trait. Are there other strong traits that will contribute to achieving the desired behavior? If you can't hire someone who is strong in absolutely all the important traits on your list, could the candidate develop the missing or weak traits through professional development after you hire them?

We've learned in our business coaching practice that many traits can be developed, though the process can be time consuming, and results can be limited. Much of our coaching work is centered on developing soft skills for leadership roles by bringing both fundamental and complementary traits to the next level. However, whether a trait is coachable or not is highly dependent on attitude. The individual must be willing to learn and be receptive to coaching.

The fact that some individuals can develop a trait doesn't necessarily mean that a particular candidate will be willing or able to do so. It's common to realize during an interview that there are certain traits an individual would need to develop or enhance to excel in a role or to advance in the organization. If so, it's important to explore the candidate's fundamental traits in the Open Mindset category, such as openness to learning, interest in learning from others, and openness to change, to ensure that the individual would be genuinely receptive.

Fit in Action: Maintaining the Focus on Key Traits

"It keeps you honest" was the feedback from a client that started using lists of fundamental and complementary traits in the hiring process. This company was interested in taking its hiring practices to the next level, especially with regard to determining the right fit. Six members of the management team who were to be involved in the interview process agreed on the fundamental and complementary traits they thought would be most important for their VP of Business Development role.

In the first interview, conducted by the hiring manager, one of the short-listed candidates conveyed excellent hard skills and also presented extremely well, was highly articulate, had a high confidence level, and demonstrated very many of the other ideal traits for the role. But this candidate didn't rate as high as the other candidates on the fundamental trait of integrity, which was a key trait required for success in the company.

In the past, this candidate would likely have been passed to the next round of interviews. However, the master lists of agreed key traits enabled the hiring manager to maintain a focus on all the important traits and not be distracted by the candidate's obvious strengths. The client was able to make a better-informed choice on fit using this trait-based screening process.

CHAPTER 8

Ensuring Fit for Senior Leadership Roles

The core elements of fit apply to all positions, including senior leadership roles. Senior leaders require a demanding combination of hard skills, such as prior leadership experience; knowledge of the legal obligations of a business; experience in the implementation of a strategic plan; and role-specific experience in such functional areas as sales, finance, or operations. They also require a broad range of soft skills—some of them quite sophisticated—that contribute to effective leadership.

In Chapter 2, we listed some complementary traits commonly needed for success in leadership roles. However, in the search for what can be difficult-to-find hard skills and sophisticated complementary traits, organizations often overlook a key component of screening for leadership success: ensuring that the candidate has the necessary fundamental traits. In screening candidates for senior leadership roles, you must avoid the temptation to take short cuts, even inadvertently, in assessing their fundamental and complementary fit traits. If you've followed our suggestions in Chapter 3, your lists of key fundamental and complementary traits for a very senior leadership role may contain as many as 30 traits in total. To make sure that you select the best-qualified candidate, you need to assess the individual for each trait in both lists.

Leadership and Fundamental Traits

For a senior leadership role, you may feel tempted to make assumptions about a candidate's fundamental traits. After all, isn't it obvious that individuals can't advance beyond a certain level in an organization without possessing the fundamental traits required of senior personnel? Well, "obvious" or not, it isn't true. Unfortunately, they can and they do, especially if organizations modify their management structure to accommodate a bad fit. Therefore, you can't assume anything about key fit traits from a candidate's level of seniority. You have to screen candidates for each trait without making allowances for the level that an individual has already reached. Of course, you need to approach senior candidates with appropriate respect for their past achievements, but don't be intimidated and don't be blinded to the need to screen for all aspects of fit.

The more senior the role, the more tempting it becomes to ignore your gut feelings. Many experienced leaders exhibit traits that can quickly color your impression of them and make you forget to complete a full assessment. Articulate communication is one such trait. You've likely met successful individuals with exceptional verbal communication skills. If you lose your focus on fit, it's easy to buy into these candidates and assume traits that they may not have.

A candidate may impress you so much with charisma, confidence, and a gift of the gab that you overlook the significance of other behaviors. For example, you might dismiss your discomfort with the candidate's body language, even though it clearly expresses arrogance or a lack of respect. By ignoring unsettling behaviors or failing to articulate your reasons for feeling uncomfortable, you may hire the wrong person. In both my executive search and career coaching practices, I've witnessed the negative consequences of zeroing in on isolated traits and drawing erroneous conclusions.

In my outplacement practice, I encounter many senior-level individuals whose organizations have let them go. In our initial encounter, they usually tell me that they left by mutual agreement. But after further discussion, I often learn about conflicts between the individual and other members of the management team. Sometimes, these conflicts have challenged the individual's limited self-management skills, leading to outbursts of anger. In most cases, the individual has fallen short, not in complementary traits but in one or more key fundamental traits. The same leader who demonstrates excellent negotiation skills in making an acquisition, for example, may have only a limited capacity to listen to peers or direct reports. Such an individual may have great ideas but be unable to put them into action because of an inability to work with others to achieve the promised results.

Dysfunctional Trickle-Down

At the senior leadership level, it becomes increasingly important to consider not only what fundamental traits the organization requires for an individual to be successful but also the impact that a particular candidate's fundamental traits might have on the organization itself. The more senior the hire, the greater is the potential impact on the organization of an individual with poor fundamental traits:

- A junior, individual contributor mainly impacts their peers.
- A vice president impacts their whole department, along with the other departments they interact with.
- A Chief Executive Officer (CEO) impacts the whole organization.

The behavior of the leader at the top of the organizational chart signals the fundamental traits the organization values. *If the leader has poor fundamental traits, the organization can experience* **dysfunctional trickle-down,** which is the transfer of poor behaviors from senior leaders to their team. This transfer is usually not intentional but results from a leader acting as a poor role model for staff. Its effects can be very serious.

Let's say you hire a CEO who's "a screamer and a shouter," using undue levels of anger to bully others and feel powerful. So does the trickle-down effect mean that the whole organization starts to copy that exact behavior? The answer is no, but staff may make assumptions about the traits the organization now values and may shift their behavior accordingly. Since displays of anger seem acceptable to the CEO, perhaps other managers may relax their own self-management skills and let themselves occasionally fly off the handle with their staff. Perhaps they may occasionally start to use profanities or show other marks of disrespect for others.

Many staff members won't contribute to the trickle-down of bad behavior, and they may thoroughly disapprove of it. These individuals may soon start to feel alienated from the emerging culture, disengage, and plan a job search. We've seen a number of cases in which the behavior of a new CEO with poor fundamental traits results in a distinct decrease in employee engagement and a significant increase in employee absenteeism and staff turnover. When such CEOs eventually leave an organization—often involuntarily—they're likely to leave behind a negative atmosphere, low morale, and a bad reputation as a place to work. This is dysfunctional trickle-down in action, and the effects can be far-reaching.

Some organizations going through a transition, such as a turnaround or amalgamation, require a positive culture change. An organization can help achieve this by selecting a top leader with traits that inspire staff to embrace a new mission and strive for higher goals. However, failing to screen such an agent of change for the fundamental traits you want to see can have very negative consequences for the organization as a whole.

You may be thinking that in order to hire a senior leader who is strong in such traits as results-orientation, assertiveness, decisiveness, and resilience, you will need to make compromises on other traits. This will be true, but you will need to decide which trade-offs are reasonable. For example, you may decide that the fundamental traits of patience, warmth, and the ability to balance work and rest are less critical than the fundamental trait of results-orientation. But it's important to make conscious decisions about trade-offs, or the end result will likely be the hiring of an individual who surprises you later with behavior you haven't bargained for.

Fit in Action: Managing Upward by Developing Traits

The traits an individual requires to succeed in some roles depend heavily on the ability to work with the personality of the boss. This relationship can be a challenge if the boss wasn't screened effectively for all the important fundamental traits. We met such a situation when we received a request for business coaching from a company in the service sector. A VP in the company worked for an effective, but unreasonably demanding, CEO who was subject to emotional mood swings and verbal outbursts. One big issue in the relationship between the CEO and the VP was that both individuals had strong opinions and wouldn't back down. They both needed to be right.

The VP was having some doubts about wanting to remain in his role. The conflict was beginning to take a toll on his enjoyment, as well as his sleep and productivity. The VP also began mirroring the CEO's behavior by yelling back when yelled at, but this response was unacceptable to the CEO and was noticed by other staff. Fortunately, the head of HR was close enough to the situation to step in. She suggested coaching as a possible solution. The CEO declined coaching, so the organization asked us to coach the VP on how to improve the relationship.

To help the VP handle the emotional mood swings of the CEO, the coaching included work on developing such complementary traits as advanced listening ability, conflict-management ability, and open communication style. By requesting coaching for the VP, the head of HR helped him to work through the challenges and avoid resigning. The VP was able to enhance his relationship with the CEO. Four years after the coaching, the two individuals were still working together effectively. However, resolving their conflict took time and money, and many such situations of dysfunctional trickle-down don't end on so positive a note.

CHAPTER 9

Structuring Interviews to Support Fit

Most roles require a significant amount of interaction with others, and the lists of key traits for most roles reflect that reality. An employee most likely needs to work effectively with a manager or supervisor and build relationships with peers and may need to work in a team with other employees from different functional areas of the organization. As you interview a candidate, you invariably have to explore the candidate's underlying relationship-building traits to assess the individual's ability to work with others in your organization. Structuring the interview process appropriately can help you do this by providing opportunities to observe the candidate's ability to interact with others under different circumstances.

The strongest candidates for a role almost always have other options. Interviewers need to ensure that the interview process effectively markets the organization and the role. The pains taken to screen candidates for fit come to naught if the best candidates gain a negative impression in the interview process and go elsewhere. As with candidate behaviors, the actions of interviewers can speak louder than words.

Involving the Right Number of Interviewers

A focused and well-run organization hires employees in a smooth and efficient way. Before the interview process begins, such an organization has mapped out the number of interviews required and the number of people required to conduct them. Indeed, if the organization is serious about fit, the interviewers have all been involved in selecting the key fit traits from the outset.

It may feel that if you interview a candidate enough times, you will eventually find enough information to determine whether the candidate is the right fit. But the reality is that organizations usually spend lots of time on interviews if they don't know clearly what they want in a candidate. As time passes, everyone, including the candidate and the individuals conducting the interviews, becomes more confused. The more people are involved, the greater the confusion.

The appropriate number of interviewers depends on the level of the role. The more senior the role, the more people need to be involved in interviewing. But there's a limit. If too many people get involved in interviewing, some candidates may conclude that the management team in an organization can't reach decisions effectively. In Table 9.1, we provide a suggested guideline for the number of interviewers required for roles at varying levels of seniority.

Table 9.1 Suggested number of interviewers, based on role seniority

Level	Number of interviewers
Manager or individual contributor	2–3
Director or VP	3–5
C-level	4–6

The individual the role reports to should conduct the organization's initial interview with each short-listed candidate, chosen on the basis of the rigorous prescreening we described in Chapter 6. By talking directly to the person they would report to, candidates can get further information about the role. Since most strong candidates already have a job, your organization can demonstrate its respect and reasonableness by demanding as little of their time as possible for the initial interview. We therefore recommend against meetings with multiple interviewers at the first-interview stage. If, after the initial interview, there's true interest from both the hiring manager and the candidate, then it's worthwhile for both parties to invest in the rest of the interview process.

Based on the best practices we've developed over many years, we recommend that interviews for a key leadership role should involve about five key stakeholders in three separate interviews of the candidate. Using this approach, organizations can make timely and efficient decisions. You may need to modify this process if key stakeholders work in different locations. To fill a VP role, for example, we suggest the following interview structure:

- **First interview:** The hiring manager interviews the candidate after the prescreening stage.
- **Second interview:** Within 2 to 4 days of the first interview, the candidate meets with two individuals from other functional areas who interact with the role. Since most leadership roles require a range of self-management and relationship-building traits, you may wish to conduct this meeting more informally—over coffee, for example—to assess the candidate's conduct in social settings. Immediately following this meeting, the candidate may have a more structured second meeting with the hiring manager, who can then gain additional insight into the candidate.
- **Third interview:** Within 2 to 3 days of the second interview, the candidate meets with the individual ranked immediately above the hiring manager and with an HR representative, if HR is involved in the process.

Undue time spent on interviews can also lead to fatigue. Managers may reach the point where they just want the process to end. At that point, they may overlook candidates' deficiencies just to move forward. Meanwhile, candidates may lose confidence in the organization's ability to make a decision. They may even drop out of contention and move on to other opportunities.

By articulating clearly, from the outset of a search, the hard and soft skills required for a role, organizations can conduct a limited number of timely and efficient interviews and reach a well-founded decision on fit.

Ensuring Optimum Scheduling

You will notice that we recommend a schedule with as little time as possible between the first, second, and third interviews. We also recommend timeliness in follow-up discussions between interviewers about candidates, so that an organization can reach a hiring decision expeditiously without leaving candidates hanging. The benefits of ensuring that the process doesn't drag on include the following:

- Your organization appears to be focused and efficient, with a collaborative leadership team, thus impressing candidates and contributing to positive word on the street.
- You maintain emotional buy-in from candidates.
- Promising candidates with other options don't withdraw from contention before you've made a selection.
- Interviewers treat the process as a high priority and retain stronger memories of candidates when engaging in follow-up discussions with other interviewers.

There are always exceptions to any rule of thumb, and so it is with our suggested sequence of interviews. For example, if an organization is hiring a CEO, the Board Chair may act as the "hiring manager," but different organizations may make different decisions on which employees and board members to include in screening. Timeliness remains important, however, and the basics of establishing fit remain the same, beginning with the lists of key traits.

Encouraging Open and Insightful Exchanges

In Chapter 7, we described how you can use curiosity and relaxed discussion to probe the reasons behind niggling feelings you may have when interviewing a candidate. But the need to encourage conversation extends beyond this context and is an important element of skilled interviewing.

The objective of a successful interview is to acquire enough information to make an informed assessment of the candidate, based on preselected key fit traits, by listening to their answers to questions and their statements in discussions and by observing their body language. Candidates will be more likely to provide full information if they feel comfortable. Therefore, an interviewer with the intention of curiosity rather than judgment will gain more insight. *When candidates feel accepted and acknowledged, they're more likely to talk freely and openly.* This is your aim so that you learn as much as possible by hearing the candidate's unguarded statements and observing the candidate's genuine behaviors.

The most successful interviewers primarily ask questions that put a candidate at ease. This is especially true at the early stages of an interview when deliberately awkward or hostile questions will put candidates on guard, restrict the information they share with you, and allow little insight into their character and motivation. In a hostile or uncomfortable setting, a candidate will volunteer only limited information and will behave atypically. Even if you succeed in getting the information you want, candidates may not be attracted to you as a peer or a boss, sensing that you might be difficult to work with. Expressing hostility and creating discomfort may also appear to reflect badly on the atmosphere in your organization.

In probing for information, there's a difference between trying to stump a person and posing a question that requires a thoughtful reply. Depending on the traits that the role requires, you may want to assess a candidate's ability to deal with questions from peers or management that require careful but immediate thought. How candidates behave in response can provide you with information on how they handle themselves when they need to think on their feet.

Questions such as "What aspect of success is most important to you?" and "If you became CEO of this company, what would you do first?" are likely to be challenging for many candidates. But there's a difference between a challenging question and a hostile one. The distinguishing factor is the overall tone of the interview, which should have a relaxed and cordial feel and should encourage open discussion. You can choose whether to ask any question in a curious or an antagonistic fashion. Choosing to use an interested, friendly tone of voice will provide you with more useful information on fit.

In Chapter 10, we will discuss in more detail the most useful initial and follow-up questions to ask a candidate to help uncover traits. But you need to do more than simply ask questions. You also need to structure the interview in a way that encourages a conversation. You want the candidate, in addition to giving basic answers to your questions, to engage with you in a fluid discussion, which will reveal information below the surface of the immediate answers. To do this, you have to put the candidate at ease from the outset of the meeting and maintain a positive atmosphere throughout. Here are some tips:

- Approach the meeting with the intention of getting to know the candidate. Remind yourself that you want to get to know the *person*, rather than simply screening a candidate.

- Set the tone of the interview as a friendly meeting. Greet the candidate with a smile, offer water, and engage in initial small talk to create a warm, open, and respectful environment.
- During the discussion, give your full attention to the candidate to express genuine interest and make the candidate feel accepted and valued. No matter what the pressures of the day are, don't permit phone calls or visits from colleagues to interrupt the meeting.
- Acknowledge the candidate's statements by nodding, smiling, and commenting appropriately to encourage openness, keeping your body relaxed to avoid sending mixed messages.

The candidates you interview should feel that you've really listened to what they've said. They should feel that you've given them every opportunity to demonstrate who they are and what they bring to the table. Not only is this the right thing to do, but it's also in your best interests as a potential peer or boss of a candidate and in the best interests of the reputation of your organization.

Fit in Action: Keeping Interview Demands within Reason

In my career consulting practice, I met a midlevel executive who was questioning whether to stay with her employer. Her experiences provided a very clear example of how an inappropriate interview structure, with too many interviews, can discourage strong internal, as well as external, candidates.

This individual had an excellent track record with the company, progressing through carefully selected roles to her executive position. She was very intelligent and had acquired the hard and soft skills needed to advance further in the company. She'd applied internally for a promotion when an opening appeared for a vice president. The role was a natural next step in her career. The timing seemed right, and she felt highly motivated to do the job well. The company's management team seemed to think so as well and put her forward as a potential candidate.

The company used a search firm for all of its hires. After proceeding through the search firm's prescreening, the internal candidate presented herself for interviews with a total of eight senior individuals in the company, who all knew her and the quality of her work. At this point, she'd invested more than 10 hours of her time on interviews and was beginning to question how the management team regarded her. Her attempts to gain feedback on her candidacy produced superficial, unclear responses, though her personal interactions with the interviewers remained positive and encouraging. During the overly protracted interview process, she began to question her future with the company. She wondered if a decision not to promote her had already been made.

The candidate came to us to try to gain insight into what was going on and to assess her readiness for a promotion. We determined that she was indeed ready for the next step in her career. And, in fact, her employer subsequently promoted her, though not to the position she'd applied for. Despite the promotion, the candidate's loyalty to the company had suffered significant damage, and she became more open to offers from competitors.

CHAPTER 10

Interview Questions That Reveal Fit

Interviews typically last for 40 to 90 minutes, so there's a limit to the number of questions you can ask. It's important that you plan some questions ahead of time to make the most effective use of the interview time and maintain your focus on fit. By the end of the interview process, you need to have a clear picture of the candidate's hard-skill fit, soft-skill fit, and expectation fit. You also need to explore and understand any niggling feelings you have about the candidate's fit with the organization or the role.

The Use of Traditional Questions

The two most common types of traditional interview questions are:

- **Informational questions**, which elicit factual responses, enabling you to gather concrete information on the breadth and depth of a candidate's hard skills. Examples include:
  - What can you tell me about your experience with financial governance?
  - How have you kept your technical skills up to date?

Candidates usually find informational questions fairly easy to address, so these questions can be useful early in an interview to relax the candidate and encourage comfortable exchanges. However, while the answers to these questions are instructive about hard-skill fit, they reveal little about soft-skill fit.

- **Situational/behavioral questions**, which are aimed at getting the candidate to talk about past behavior to reveal information for assessing soft-skill fit. Examples include:

○ Can you tell me about a time when you stalled on a project or task? What steps did you take to address the problem, and what was the outcome?

○ Have you had staff who were dissatisfied with their jobs? How did their dissatisfaction express itself, and how did you handle the situation?

○ Have you ever been given confidential information that made you uncomfortable? What did you do with the information?

Some candidates have difficulty in answering this type of question. They may be thrown off balance and may struggle to find the words they need for a suitable answer. They may clam up initially and then blurt out a few tentative sentences that convey little information of value. They may also become very uncomfortable, and their discomfort may then affect their behavior and the amount of information they volunteer for the remainder of the interview. Other candidates may have thoroughly prepared themselves in advance for such questions and deliver rehearsed answers that give you little insight into fit.

A further limitation of behavioral questions is their focus on past behavior. The candidate may have developed considerably in the time since that behavior took place. Also, the candidate may not have been free to act in the way they would have liked. They may have behaved in a certain way because they were required to, not because they saw the course of action as the most reasonable or most effective.

To obtain really useful information for assessing soft-skill fit, you need to take a different approach to exploring a candidate's behavior. *You can learn more about the candidate by finding out how they feel about situations and how they would behave if they were free to choose a course of action.* And, of course, you can learn a good deal about some of the candidate's self-management, relationship-building, and presentation traits by direct observation of the candidate's behaviors.

The Advantage of Revealing Questions

Revealing questions, which are open-ended, encourage individuals to talk about themselves freely. In the process, they're much more likely to reveal their true personality, style, and motivation.

- What qualities in your coworkers bother you the most? What qualities do you appreciate most in others?
- What is the easiest/most difficult part of your present role? Why?
- What work setting have you liked the most? Why?
- What kind of support would you need to be successful in this role?
- If you could change anything about your present role, what would it be?
- If you were hiring a direct report, what personal qualities would you most look for?
- How would you handle a direct report who seems unable to take direction?

With good questions, you can gain lots of information about a candidate. Candidates' answers may also raise red flags about their suitability for a role. But even then, you may not receive enough information to make a sound decision about fit. To determine whether you need more insight into a candidate's fit, analyze the candidate's response to a revealing question by asking yourself the following questions:

- Did the response seem genuine, honest, and straightforward?
- Did the response seem superficial?
- Did the response seem to contradict other information from the candidate's résumé or other sources?
- Did the response seem to be at odds with the candidate's body language?

Questions That Probe Deeper

When you feel a need to question a candidate more deeply, you might ask the following types of questions. Again, the aim is to allow open-ended responses.

- Can you tell me more about that?
- How do you feel about that?
- What might your other options be?
- What other ideas/feelings do you have about it?

- How do you think your colleagues would respond to that idea?
- What result would you predict?
- What additional support would you need to accomplish that?

When your intuition tells you that you're not getting the full story, you may wish to ask such questions as:

- If that approach/method/action failed, what would you do then? If after listening to the response you're still unsatisfied, you might then ask:
- And if that alternate approach/method/action also didn't work, what would you do then?

Checking Motivation and Career Path Compatibility

To ensure fit, you also need to make sure that the candidate's motivation and career goals are compatible with your organization's expectations of performance in the role and opportunities for advancement. A preliminary assessment of expectation fit should have been part of prescreening, as described in Chapter 6. The interview stage should include a thorough, direct assessment of motivation and career path compatibility. You can do this by asking the candidate a variety of questions. Informational questions can help provide some important background and set a relaxed tone.

To assess motivation compatibility, you might ask such informational questions as:

- What is the most/least interesting part of your current role?
- How would you describe your interpersonal relationships in your current role?

The answers to revealing questions can provide more insight into motivation compatibility, as well as adding to the picture of the candidate's traits:

- What would you expect to give back to the organization?
- What most motivates you to excel?
- What aspect of success is most important to you?

Possible informational questions for checking career path compatibility include:

- How have you managed your career to ensure that you've grown professionally?
- Has mentoring helped you in your career? How?
- What opportunities for promotion would you ideally like and when?
- What development and training opportunities would you ideally like?

Possible revealing questions for checking career path compatibility include:

- Are you satisfied with your career path to date? If you could have changed anything about it, what would it have been?
- If your career were progressing more slowly than you wanted, what would you do?
- What is your biggest career achievement to date? Why do you think so?

There's no sharp division between questions that explore motivation compatibility and those that explore career path compatibility. For example, a candidate's views about success in answer to the third revealing question on motivation may also shed light on career path expectations. A candidate's description of a career achievement in response to the third revealing question on career path may also clarify the candidate's motivation.

Your assessment of motivation and career path compatibility should be part of your decision on whether to move ahead with a candidate. Defining the potential career path and development opportunities that the role offers should have been part of the organization's forward planning for filling the role. But after clarifying the candidate's goals, there's sometimes uncertainty over whether the organization can satisfy them. If so, you will need to obtain clarification of the career path that the organization can provide. You must ensure that there's real compatibility between the candidate's and the organization's expectations before you consider whether to make an offer.

Checking Compensation, Location, and Work-Demands Compatibility

As mentioned in Chapters 5 and 6, the first discussion about compensation, location, and work demands should take place at the prescreening stage. A second conversation needs to take place during the interview stage, in preparation for a possible offer. This midstage conversation can be conducted by HR or the hiring manager or by an executive search firm if you're using one.

The topic of compensation can be emotionally charged, so we suggest prefacing the first question with a statement that provides a context. A possible preface might be:

> You provided us with some earlier information about compensation, and I want to find out a little more about what elements are most important to you at this time in your career. I'm not looking to negotiate a compensation package just yet, as we haven't completed the interview process, but I want to have an overall sense of your interests in the event that both of us would like to move forward.

An informational question regarding compensation might then be:

- Could you let me know how your compensation in your last role was structured? Besides the base salary and bonus, did you receive any other perks?

Revealing questions regarding compensation might be:

- How satisfied were you with your last compensation package?
- What would be most important to you in terms of compensation elements if you were to join our organization?

Location and work demands are typically less sensitive topics than compensation, but candidates may have personal preferences or family situations that make these aspects of the role very important. You must thoroughly assess the degree of compatibility.

Informational questions regarding location might include:

- Was your last job close to home? How long was the commute?
- Have you had a job with a long commute or one that required significant travel? How much of your time did they take?

Revealing questions about location might include:

- How do you feel about the commuting/travel requirements of the role?
- Do you foresee any challenges with the commuting/travel requirements of the role?

An informational question regarding work demands might be:

- What was the greatest pressure point in your most recent role? For how much of the year did you have to deal with it?

Revealing questions regarding work demands might include:

- Now that you have a sense of the role, which parts of it would you expect to take the majority of your time? Do you think that the answer would be different at different times of the year?
- What do you think would be the greatest pressure point in the role? When dealing with this pressure point, how would you deal with aspects of the role that are not as critical but still need attention?

Ensuring Interviewer Preparation

Since the hiring manager alone commonly conducts the first interview, it's important for the manager to prepare thoroughly, in order both to screen the candidate effectively and to make a positive impression. In addition to being aware of the general types of questions described previously, the manager needs to prepare questions that explore specific fundamental and complementary traits selected for the role. However, time constraints won't permit the manager to ask questions on every trait, so selectivity is important. Fortunately, many traits are apparent from direct observation of the candidate's behaviors, and *questioning can focus on traits that are harder to identify.*

Suppose, for example, that among the required traits are accountability, responsiveness, integrity, friendliness, confidence, persuasiveness, and planning ability. The hiring manager is likely to gain a great deal of information about the candidate's responsiveness, friendliness, confidence, and persuasiveness by observing behaviors and listening to the answers to a wide variety of questions. But it's much harder to use direct observation to get a sense of the traits of accountability, integrity, and planning ability within the limitations of an interview, so trait-related questions might most productively concentrate on those traits.

For example, the trait of **accountability** can be defined as an obligation or willingness to accept responsibility for or to account for one's actions. Before the interview, the manager is likely to gain some insight into a candidate's accountability by reflecting on behaviors observed in prescreening:

- Does the individual submit documents promptly or make excuses for late delivery?
- Does the individual adhere to schedules for phone calls?
- Does the individual accept responsibility for any omissions or lack of clarity in the initial application letter or in responses to e-mail or phone prescreening questions?

In the first interview, the manager can determine the candidate's level of accountability more precisely by asking informational and revealing questions and being curious about the responses.

- What aspects of your current role do you take responsibility for? What isn't your responsibility? Why isn't it?
- In your last performance review, what areas were flagged for development? Did you feel that the comments were valid? How did you respond at the time? What have you done to develop in these areas since then?
- What are you responsible for in your role? What is your boss responsible for? What is your feeling about the division of duties?

- If a direct report made a serious mistake, what would you do?
- If your boss denied responsibility for a poor decision that affected your work performance, how would you handle the situation?
- Do you think that all employees should be equally accountable for their work performance?

When necessary to gain more insight, perhaps following a superficial response, the manager should interject appropriate questions that encourage the candidate to talk more and provide more detail:

- Can you tell me more about that?
- Why do you think that?
- When is it your responsibility, and when isn't it?
- How did your boss respond to that? Did you agree with your boss's response?

When listening to the candidate's answers, the manager should watch for signs in the individual's words or body language to indicate unauthentic replies and should follow up with deeper questions when necessary:

- If your boss didn't agree, would you try to convince her? How would you do that
- If that approach didn't work, would you try a different approach? If so, what would that be?

Always keep in mind that the answers to questions targeted at a particular trait are likely to shed light on other traits. For example, if the candidate is describing what his or her reactions would be to a serious error by a direct report, the interviewer may well gain insight into such traits as integrity, empathy, reasonableness, and judgment, as well as accountability.

After the interview, the hiring manager should analyze the responses and record assessments of the candidate's traits in Tables 3.1 and 3.3, the fundamental and complementary traits rating tables containing the key traits chosen in Chapter 3. The manager should note any unresolved red flags, such as incongruent body language or contradictory statements. A meeting of all the interviewers to discuss the outcome of the first interview may result in the elimination of a candidate or a decision to screen further in a second interview. If there's a second interview, the hiring manager can use the opportunity to meet with the candidate again at the end of the interview. The manager can then explore any issues remaining from the first interview, as well as covering new ground, and can look for and *explore any inconsistencies in statements or behaviors from one interview to the next.*

Each interviewer other than the hiring manager is likely to meet the candidate only once, so these other interviewers have less opportunity to follow up on unresolved issues or observe the candidate's behaviors in different settings. It's likely that the other interviewers will mainly explore traits most relevant to their own areas of responsibility.

For example, suppose a company is hiring a Director of Finance. The group of interviewers includes the Chief Operating Officer (COO) and the Director of HR, in addition to the CFO, who is the hiring manager. These individuals were all involved in selecting the agreed lists of key fundamental and complementary traits for the director role, so those lists reflect their individual priorities to some extent.

The COO may well be most interested in cross-functional aspects of the director's role and may value such traits as responsiveness, co-operativeness, respect for the opinions of others, willingness to share information, and collaborative approach. Assuming that the agreed lists include these traits, the COO might want to concentrate on exploring them in the limited time available.

The Director of HR, on the other hand, might be most interested in exploring the agreed key traits that would most contribute to the individual's fit with the corporate culture to become a respected and fully integrated member of the company. These might include team-orientation, sense of social and business etiquette, political savvy, and commitment to business ethics. Both the COO and the Director of HR should prepare for the interview by devising questions that explore the less easily recognized of the traits they wish to explore.

To ensure consistency and clear communication, all interviewers must record their assessments of the candidate's traits in Tables 3.1 and 3.3, which contain the agreed lists of fundamental and complementary traits.

To ensure the accuracy and completeness of the information, it's best to record the assessments and note any red flags immediately after each interview, while the information is fresh in the interviewers' minds. The next stage in our TAP will be to combine the individual assessments of the candidate into an overall assessment.

Fit in Action: Digging Deeper Pays Dividends

A multinational organization asked us to identify candidates with strong managerial skills to fill a director's position. A large number of staff reported to the director, and the company expected the successful candidate to spend time coaching and mentoring employees. This expectation was in keeping with the company's carefully monitored culture of long-term employment and staff retention.

In compiling our long list, we identified an impressive candidate who appeared to demonstrate many of the key hard and soft skills required for the role. She seemed motivated to move into the job and was enthusiastic about the location of the office and comfortable with the general compensation range.

In the interview, she demonstrated key traits that the client was looking for, such as confidence, accuracy, decision-making ability, and the ability to deliver relevant information. However, when we asked for her thoughts about managing staff, her initial replies seemed superficial, so we probed deeper. We asked how she would respond to employees who seemed unable to take direction. Again receiving a superficial answer, we twice asked what she would do if her initial suggestions didn't work. The candidate's body language suggested that she seemed irritated by the questions. She looked away and grimaced. Then she glared at us and said, "Just fire them."

For obvious reasons, we concluded that this candidate would have difficulty in adapting to different personality types within the company and would fall short in mentoring staff. We didn't add her name to our short list.

CHAPTER 11

Reaching a Consensus on Fit

Before making a final decision on the successful candidate, the hiring manager needs to hear all the feedback from all the other interviewers about each candidate.

Discussion Pointers after Interviewing

Your discussion of the candidates, based on the assessments recorded for the fundamental and complementary traits in Tables 3.1 and 3.3, and on any red flags you noted, should address the following questions:

- What red flags did the interviews uncover?
- Did interviewers receive contradictory information that they failed to clarify in the interview? (For example, did a candidate say one thing but express another with body language?)
- Does another interviewer have the information that you lack? Does it address all of your concerns?
- How did each interviewer react instinctively to each candidate? How does each interviewer explain the particular gut feel about a candidate in relation to the candidate's traits?
- Does a particular candidate seem too weak in one or more key traits? Are the traits coachable, and can the organization take the time for the candidate to come up to speed on these traits? Does the candidate have the traits needed for coaching to be successful?
- Did any of the interviewers consider a particular trait of the candidate to be a showstopper?
- Are there any questions about the compatibility of the candidate's and the organization's expectations? Do the role and the organization make sense in terms of the candidate's motivation and career aspirations?

- Are there any uncertainties about compatibility concerning compensation, location, or work demands?
- Have you acquired all the necessary information about each candidate, or do you need more information about a particular individual?

During the discussions of the interviews, differences of opinion may well arise about candidates. These differences are often relatively minor, if everyone has agreed in advance on the key hiring traits. The hiring manager needs to listen to and assess the opinions of others, but in most cases the hiring manager should make the final decision about the preferred candidate.

The Question of Personality Tests

In our executive search and career coaching practices, we've observed both the productive use and the misuse of personality tests. At their best, they provide additional personality trait information that can be incorporated into a thorough examination of fit. At their worst, they're used in isolation from the broader considerations of fit and contribute to unreliable hiring decisions. The function of poorly used personality tests sometimes appears to be largely political, providing cover for indecision when the time comes to select the successful candidate.

Perhaps as you've been reading this book, you've asked yourself, "Why don't I screen for hard skills myself and use a personality test to determine soft-skill fit?" On the surface, this may seem like an easy and reasonable approach. But even the best personality tests, if used with insufficient context, won't determine fit. They may shed light on the personality of the candidate, but they can't determine whether the individual is a fit for a *particular role* in your organization. Nor can they provide a full assessment of the candidate's compatibility with the corporate culture, values, and objectives. Furthermore, personality tests can't determine whether the individual's motivation and career path, compensation, location, or work-demands expectations align with what the organization and the role can offer.

To establish fit, you must assess the candidate in relation to the fundamental and complementary traits needed to succeed in the organization and the specific role. You must also assess the candidate's motivation and career path, compensation, location, and work-demands expectations. Without clearly identifying the fit from both the organization's and the candidate's perspectives, you can't establish fit in the screening process. This statement is true whether you use personality tests or not.

Candidates often undergo personality testing online by means of a self-assessment. However, as we indicated earlier, actions speak louder than words. Even within the limitations of an interview, the observed behaviors of the candidate are far superior to verbal responses as indicators of many traits and as predictors of future success. Assuming you use a quality test—and many are not—you need to interpret the results carefully in the context of everything you know about the candidate. You shouldn't let the test results take on a life of their own, without regard to your other observations.

If the test results raise red flags that you're unable to resolve using what you already know, you always have the option of an additional discussion with the candidate to explore your concerns. In the uncommon event that such a discussion is necessary, it should be scheduled as soon as possible after the testing. For reasons described in Chapter 9, you should avoid a protracted interview process or a lengthy delay in reaching a decision.

Overall, then, personality tests can be used as one tool in determining fit, but only if they're taken as part of the evidence for the candidate's traits, which must also be assessed through prescreening and interviews in relation to the traits you need. However, we've found through years of experience that the thorough application of the approach described in this book can establish fit without the need for personality testing.

The Value and Limitations of References

As with the use of personality tests in determining fit, it's essential to consider the information gained from employment references in the context of all the information gathered in prescreening and the interview process. References may uncover some potential red flags that need exploring, or they may provide new insight or additional information about the individual. However, a degree of caution is required in interpreting references. How an individual performed in a previous job may not be an accurate indicator of how they will fare in a very different organizational culture and role.

References from more recent employment provide more up-to-date information about the candidate, but references covering a greater time span provide information on how, or whether, the candidate has grown and matured.

When checking references, it's useful to:

- Confirm that information on the candidate's résumé is accurate, including the dates of employment, the level and type of responsibility, and the skills the role required
- Obtain additional information about the learning that took place during the tenure of the role
- Obtain information about the candidate's actual behaviors in specific previous situations
- Gain an understanding of how the individual has responded to feedback in the past

Unfortunately, many referees deliberately provide little detail and share only superficial information. This may be for a variety of reasons, including:

- The organization or the individual referee may have concerns about possible legal action relating to defamation.
- Candidates may have chosen referees most inclined to omit or downplay any negative information.
- Referees may only have partial information and a limited perspective on the candidate.
- Information that relies on memory may be limited, especially for roles held some years ago.

To gain as much insight into the individual as possible, it's important to conduct reference checks in an optimal fashion, as outlined in the next two sections.

Information from the Reference List

In our experience, the greatest value of the reference process lies in the response to the initial step, requesting a reference list from the candidate. In our executive search practice, we request it early in the interview stage of the process, as the response can be very enlightening.

Typically, a candidate with a strong track record is comfortable providing the names of their bosses, peers, and staff from their last three previous employers. Willingly offering these names suggests that the candidate had positive relationships throughout those organizations.

If a candidate's reference list bypasses one or more key stakeholders in a previous role, you now have a great opportunity to dig deeper and find out why the names you expected to see aren't there. When you ask about omissions, you may observe the candidate look away or squirm if this is an uncomfortable subject. Indifferent or vague responses, such as "I've lost track of that person," "I think they retired," or "I think they left the country," require some additional digging. There's the possibility that the candidate didn't maintain the relationships because they weren't that positive.

However, there may be valid reasons for not including key stakeholders, such as a former boss, in the reference list. A less-than-perfect relationship may have been more to do with the character and behavior of the boss than with the qualities of the direct report. So rather than judging this situation superficially, you can use the opportunity for a more in-depth conversation about why the candidate isn't using a particular boss as a reference. This conversation can be a productive way to gain further insight into the fundamental traits of the candidate, such as confidence, self-control, honesty, respect for the opinions of others, and willingness to share information.

Using Appropriate Questions in Reference Checks

Whether you conduct reference checks yourself or through an outside party, they provide an opportunity to ask additional questions about a candidate's behaviors in an actual work setting. As with the interview process, the *reference checks need to penetrate beneath the superficial level in order to uncover valuable additional information.* The information you receive in the references will either confirm your impression of the candidate or show contradictions that may need further investigation. There may, of course, be contradictions between one reference and another for the same candidate.

In addition to checking general information that the candidate provided, you're likely to focus on the past behaviors and achievements that are most relevant to the requirements of the new role. If, for example, the new role places a premium on the traits of analytical ability and autonomy, you can ask questions that explore the extent to which the candidate has demonstrated these traits in the past. Such questions can be very direct, such as:

- How important was analytical work in the role?
- How proficient was he or she at completing analytical tasks?
- How much day-to-day supervision did you find that he or she needed?

You may wish to use questions that parallel some of those you asked the candidate in an interview. In this way, you can gain the perspective of both the candidate and an employer on the same topic and build a picture of the accuracy of the candidate's statements concerning past behaviors, levels of responsibility, and achievements. Here are some examples of parallel interview (I) and reference (R) questions:

I: What level of autonomy did you have in decision making in the role?

R: What level of autonomy did he or she have in decision making in the role?

I: In what ways did the role develop during your tenure? How responsible were you for those developments?

R: In what ways did the role develop during his or her tenure? How responsible was he or she for those developments?

I: What was the most difficult part of your role? Why?

R: What do you think he or she found was the most difficult part of his or her role? Why do you think he or she found it difficult?

I: What kind of support did you need from your boss to be successful in your role?

R: What kind of support did you need to provide for him or her to be successful in his or her role?

I: What do you think was the most important formal or informal feedback you received from your boss? How did you use the feedback in your professional growth?

R: What do you think was the most important formal or informal feedback you provided to him or her? How did he or she use the feedback in his or her professional growth?

As with a candidate in an interview, putting a referee at ease and having a relaxed exchange will pay dividends in the quality and amount of information you receive. The use of probing follow-up questions can open up the conversation and allow you to uncover information until you feel satisfied with the answers. As in interviews, it's important to use the same approach of curiosity and genuine interest in learning more, rather than going through a rote question-and-answer process.

Examples of follow-up questions intended to encourage a free-flowing conversation might include:

- That sounds interesting. Can you tell me more about how he or she was able to do that?
- And how did his or her colleagues respond to that idea?
- And why do you think that happened?

If, as in the case of personality tests, you use references to gain additional insight into a candidate, then it's equally important to interpret them carefully in the light of what you already know about the candidate. If absolutely necessary, you can promptly follow up with the candidate to resolve any issues that remain and to facilitate a timely decision.

Fit in Action: Getting the Full Picture

A top short-listed candidate for a Director of Sales search was asked by the client to undertake a self-assessment personality test. While the majority of the traits required for the role were evident in the assessment, a trait on which the candidate had a low score in the test was warmth. This isolated low score led the client to assume initially that the candidate had poor interpersonal skills.

On surface examination, this conclusion might seem valid. However, the trait of warmth is only one of the many traits in the toolbox of relationship building. Other relationship-building traits include cooperativeness, fairness, honesty, positive attitude, sense of social and business etiquette, team-orientation, and willingness to share information. And the individual had high scores on these other traits.

Further discussion and exploration with this candidate uncovered his strong self-awareness and his openness to learning and coaching. While confessing to not being a "touchy-feely" person by nature, he'd learned from mentoring and coaching to temper his approach by listening more deeply and becoming more responsive to the concerns and issues of others. Armed with this learning, he'd combined his type-A personality and strong management skills with his increased awareness of himself and others to enhance his leadership skills. As a result, he'd become a very successful leader who was well regarded by his direct reports and other staff.

CHAPTER 12

Avoiding Hiring Pitfalls

In previous chapters, you've seen how you can identify, evaluate, and hire candidates who fit your organization and the role that you need to fill. However, in inexperienced hands, misguided assumptions can undermine the hiring-for-fit process. Avoiding hiring pitfalls is easier if you're able to identify, discuss, and dispel misguided assumptions at the outset of your search.

This chapter describes common hiring pitfalls and provides questions to help you assess your thinking, examine your hiring processes, and stay on track to a successful hiring outcome.

Pitfall 1: Overfocusing on Hard Skills

Throughout this book, you've learned about the importance of looking beyond a candidate's hard skills to evaluate fit. Hard skills acquired through education and previous experience are important. But soft skills are critical. They're based on a vast array of traits that underlie a candidate's personality, values, capabilities, and leadership capacities. Previous chapters have focused on these traits and the ways in which you can identify and assess them in a candidate.

Unfortunately, it requires time and effort to identify soft skills accurately, especially those that rely on a complex array of traits. It takes far less time and effort to identify a candidate's hard skills. They're typically front and center in a candidate's résumé, and most interviewers have little difficulty in asking questions about them.

As mentioned in Chapter 1, we see most hiring managers screening primarily for hard skills at the expense of the critical soft-skill traits needed for success in the organization and the role. This is why searches often fail to identify the right hire.

While certain hard skills are essential for a role, many are of lesser importance and can be readily acquired by motivated hires. For example, a search for a controller of a large company might well require a facility with ERP systems, but requiring extensive experience with any one particular system will greatly limit the pool of candidates and therefore reduce the likelihood of finding the right soft-skill fit.

Requiring easily learned hard skills ignores a common trait among the strongest performers in an organization—a motivation to learn. In fact, successful hires will keep developing their hard skills anyway, as their role changes and grows over time.

It may feel like common sense to select the candidate whose hard skills correspond most closely to all your hard-skill requirements for a role. But this candidate may be lacking in other ways. If new hires fall short of expectations, it's seldom because they lack hard skills; most often, it's because their soft skills don't fit the organization or the role.

You might consider the following questions to decide whether you're paying sufficient attention to candidates' soft skills:

- Have you focused in your initial screening only on candidates' hard skills?
- Have you required so many or such specific hard skills that the pool of eligible candidates is very small?
- Have you clearly identified the key soft-skill traits needed for success in the organization and the role?
- In screening potential candidates, have you required so many hard skills that you've disqualified individuals who have sufficient hard skills, the ability to learn more, and the traits needed to succeed in the organization and the role?
- Have you maintained a focus on soft skills throughout the search, up to and including the selection of the successful candidate?

Pitfall 2: Limiting Your Search to Same-Sector Candidates

At first glance, a hire from the same sector may seem preferable, since the individual already has some desirable knowledge. But sector knowledge may not be sufficient to ensure that a candidate will succeed in your organization or the role you are filling. You might assume that a candidate with experience in the same sector as yours will fit readily into your organization. After all, the candidate already understands the dynamics of the sector. And you might also assume that, with experience of the sector, the candidate has the right soft-skill traits for the role.

But different organizations operate in different ways, whether they're in the same sector or not. To succeed in a role in your organization, a candidate's soft skills have to fit your requirements. A candidate from a different sector, with sufficient transferable hard skills, may have a closer match of soft skills with the requirements of your organization and the role, even if the individual knows less about the sector in which your organization operates than a same-sector candidate. A motivated hire from another sector can readily acquire this sector-specific knowledge. Indeed, he or she has already shown the ability to do so in a different sector. If you focus only on same-sector candidates, you will unnecessarily limit your chances of finding a great soft-skill fit.

The following questions may help you consider whether you're open to candidates from other sectors:

- In specifying qualifications and experience, have you limited your potential candidates to individuals within the same sector? Could someone from another sector possibly meet your requirements?
- In discussing the search with key stakeholders, have you reached a consensus on considering candidates from other sectors with the necessary transferable hard skills and the required soft skills for the role?
- In screening candidates, have you made the unverified assumption that experience in your sector implies that a candidate has certain hard and soft skills?
- In making your final selection of the successful candidate, have you favored same-sector candidates irrespective of their soft-skill fit?

Pitfall 3: Assuming That a Matching Title Guarantees Fit

It may seem that a candidate who has occupied the same role in another organization will be well equipped to perform it in yours. But as previous chapters have discussed, what candidates have done matters less than the way in which they've done it. Candidates with a title that matches the available role in your organization may have the experience you prefer, but they're not necessarily good at what they do, and there's no guarantee that they will fit the role in your organization. They may be poor communicators, for example, or they may not work well with others, and your organization may place greater emphasis on these requirements than does the candidate's present employer. You always need to evaluate soft skills in your prescreening and interviews to see if candidates fit the organization and the role, even if candidates appear to have the experience you're looking for because of their current job titles. Your evaluation will determine whether a candidate has the right soft-skill traits required to succeed.

If you want to hire an adaptable individual for a role that will grow and evolve over time, you should be wary of candidates who apply for a role that they're already performing in another organization. *Strong performers don't usually move from one organization to another unless they're advancing in their careers.* They welcome new challenges and seek roles that are a step up.

You might consider the following questions to help avoid the matching-title pitfall:

- Do titles and experience matter more in your selection process than soft skills, performance, and track record?
- In drawing up a short list, do you give preference to candidates with the same title as the role you're looking to fill?
- Do you make assumptions about a candidate's soft skills on the basis of the candidate's existing role and title?
- After screening candidates for the essential traits, do you revert to favoring matching-title candidates, irrespective of soft-skill fit?

Pitfall 4: Admitting Senior Leaders Late in the Search Process

Presidents, CEOs, and Board members can provide valuable input and perspective to the search process if they join the search team at the outset; contribute to the development of the search criteria; and apply the same criteria as the rest of the search team in identifying, evaluating, and selecting candidates. But some senior leaders choose to get involved at a later stage of the process, not until final interviews in some cases, and they can then do more harm than good.

Unless they've been involved from the outset, their search priorities and evaluation criteria will not be aligned with those of the rest of the search team. In addition, they may hold and apply uninformed views of the hiring process, such as relying on an overemphasis on hard skills or showing a lack of insight into assessing soft-skill fit. Because of the power they hold, these senior individuals may well prevail in imposing their criteria on the search at a late stage, impeding and perhaps entirely thwarting the search team's efforts. In the worst cases, the team may have to revise its selection of final candidates or even start the hiring process all over again.

Trying to deter a senior leader from joining a search at a late stage can require considerable political courage from the hiring manager. This challenge is best avoided by addressing the following questions at the outset of the search:

- Have you invited input about the role in question from all stakeholders working directly with it, including senior leaders?
- Have you given senior executives, board members, and especially the individual to whom you report an opportunity to join the hiring process?
- Do you have agreement from senior leaders that no one can join the search team after the start of the search?

Pitfall 5: Abandoning Your Leadership Role

In my experience, it's not uncommon for hiring managers to delegate responsibility for hiring a candidate and then remove themselves completely from the hiring process. This degree of delegation seldom happens in other important functions of an organization where leadership is required, such as strategic planning or organizational restructuring.

The consequences of abandoning the leadership role can be disastrous. Without firm leadership directing the development of the search team, the search criteria, and the candidate-screening process, the search team may be ill-defined, and its members may move in different directions as they use different criteria and screening processes to select candidates. Team members may reach different, and perhaps completely incompatible, conclusions about the most suitable candidates.

As a result of conflicting views, the search process may take longer than necessary or may default to weak search criteria, such as an overreliance on hard skills or previous experience. In the face of time delays and a lack of clarity over the nature of the role, strong candidates may lose interest, accept an offer from a different organization, or turn down your offer when you finally present it.

Your search team may include competent interviewers from the C-suite and the most capable people from your internal Human Resources Department, perhaps in association with a highly qualified search firm. Input from each team member is critical, but the team will function effectively only if you present the initial overview of the hiring process and guide the team through each stage. *With your leadership, everyone on the team will agree from the outset on the nature and requirements of the role and the criteria and processes that the team will follow in identifying, evaluating, and selecting candidates.*

As a leader, you will inevitably delegate responsibility for day-to-day activities of the search team. But only you can provide the consistent leadership required to keep the team focused on and adhering to the process to which all members have agreed.

To ensure that you maintain the level of leadership required for a successful search, you might consider these questions:

- Do you and your team clearly understand your role as leader in the hiring process?
- Have you and your team discussed and resolved any conflicting views about the hiring process before it begins?
- Have you clearly identified the tasks in the hiring process that you can delegate to other members of the team, as well as the tasks that you must perform yourself?
- Have you allocated sufficient time in your schedule to perform the leadership tasks required of you during a timely search?

Fit in Action: Undermining a Search

We were asked by the Board of a Property and Casualty Insurance company to provide business coaching to its new CEO. After 3 months in the role, the CEO was having trouble establishing credibility. The Board had become aware of discontent within the management team, and it appeared that the new CEO hadn't been able to build trust with the group. There were rumblings that a couple of valued long-term members of the management team were considering leaving.

For the first time in its history, the organization had conducted an external search for the new CEO. Previous CEOs had been groomed from within the company, but this time no one had been ready to assume the job. The company faced new regulatory pressures and had to adapt to the digital era, and the CEO would need to play a critical role in this transformation.

The company had conducted an extensive targeted search and used a search firm to screen for a short list of candidates. According to the Board Chair, the internal search team felt that the short list was strong. All five of the candidates had a background in financial services, two from insurance and three from the broader financial services sector. The candidates interviewed well and demonstrated strong leadership skills. They possessed the necessary core hard skills to address change management, risk management, and business development, as well as the critical soft skills required for the position, such as forward-thinking ability, adaptability, drive, respect for the opinions of others, and the ability to motivate others through change. The search had moved forward smoothly until the final stage.

At this point, one Board member, who had not been part of the internal search team, voiced his strong opinion that the short list was inadequate. He insisted that the new hire should come specifically from the Property and Casualty sector. Because this opinion came from a long-term Board member, the Board Chair felt compelled to ask the search firm to add a candidate from the Property and Casualty sector to the short list. The search firm had already targeted this specific group, but in assessing potential candidates had concluded that none were in the same league as others on the short list. Nevertheless, under pressure from the Board, the search firm presented the best B-list candidate, who had extensive experience in Property and Casualty but had a poor track record.

The company held final interviews with two candidates, one from the search firm's original short list of A-candidates, the other the B-list candidate with experience in the Property and Casualty sector. The Board overlooked this candidate's poor track record and selected him because of his knowledge of the sector. Three months into the job, it had become evident that the new hire didn't have the soft skills to do the job and couldn't adapt to the requirements of his new position.

At the request of the Board Chair, we provided the CEO with some business coaching, but we advised the Chair that coaching would have only limited impact over the short term. As we discovered in our sessions with him, the CEO, after a long career with one company, had found it difficult to adapt to CEO roles in two other Property and Casualty companies. He initially cited Board issues as the reason, but our coaching discussions uncovered many underdeveloped fundamental and complementary traits, including respect for the opinions of others, willingness to share information, openness to change, self-control, and adaptability. He exhibited a strong drive for results, an in-depth knowledge of the business, and strong business acumen, but, with such underdeveloped soft skills, he was having difficulty in building trusted relationships with his team.

The company's search had failed for two reasons. First, the search team admitted a senior leader at a late stage and was forced at the last minute to expand the short list to include an unqualified candidate. Second, the Board had assumed that a candidate with experience in the same sector would succeed in the role, whether or not he possessed the soft skills needed for the job. Unfortunately for the company, the Board was mistaken.

CHAPTER 13

Protecting Your Investment

By the time the interviewers reach a consensus on fit, as described in Chapter 11, you should have completed the first 12 steps shown in the Hiring-for-Fit Checklist, which appears as Supplement 1 at the end of this book. You're now ready to make an offer to the successful candidate. If you've had transparent discussions with the candidate about your respective expectations and repeatedly monitored the candidate's motivation, there should be no surprise in the candidate's response to the offer.

Unfortunately, *many managers seem to think that the hiring process ends when the successful candidate arrives for the first day's work.* This view makes it difficult for even the most talented individual to adjust to a new organizational culture. By abandoning newly hired individuals without providing formal training or mentoring, an organization invites problems. After selecting and hiring the successful candidate as the right fit, the organization needs to maintain and grow that fit. To do this successfully, the organization must monitor and support the individual to facilitate adjustment to the new setting.

New hires often have to deal with challenges that have little or nothing to do with the actual jobs for which they were hired. Hiring managers may also face a range of unexpected challenges in dealing with new hires.

Here are two examples of challenges that a new hire may face:

- The new boss, so happy to have an extra pair of hands, downloads part of her role to the new hire. The new hire may now have work he didn't sign up for, and he doesn't have time to develop the all-important relationships in the early weeks. As a result, he makes a poor first impression within his department and across the organization.
- The organization is moving at such a fast pace that the new boss just isn't around for the first few weeks. Although it may have been

her intention to mentor and train, year-end pressures, vacation time, or business travel requirements prevent her from supporting the new hire appropriately. Without guidance and feedback, the new hire is likely to flounder.

Here are two examples of challenges that a hiring manager may face in dealing with a new hire:

- In an attempt to create a good impression by immediately adding value, the new hire tries to change things that don't need changing now—or at all. Without guidance, the new hire sizes up the new setting too quickly to develop a clear understanding of its needs. Based on his previous setting, where he had the experience and authority to make effective changes, the new hire assumes that his new boss will welcome the change initiatives.
- The new hire isn't interacting in the expected way. During the interview process, he seemed so friendly, straightforward, and enthusiastic, but now he's not demonstrating those same traits, and he's not building sufficiently positive relationships.

An individual's initial few weeks in a role are critical in setting the stage for success. In our executive search practice, we frequently see the dividends that result when employers pay great attention to this period of transition.

Onboarding

Coaching-based onboarding can be highly effective in ensuring that the transition of the new hire into the organization is successful in cementing the fit that you've already established. Many organizations have an orientation program, which they sometimes call onboarding, but there are significant differences between an orientation program and a coaching-based onboarding program.

A typical orientation program:

- Communicates information needed by all new hires, no matter what the new role, and doesn't deal with role-specific issues

- Presents top-down information without input from the new hire
- Is a one-time event

A coaching-based onboarding program:

- Provides support for the unique challenges that arise when a new hire joins the organization
- Includes the active involvement of both the hiring manager and the new hire to make sure that the onboarding program addresses their respective needs in achieving a smooth transition
- Takes place over a period of time. It typically begins before the start date to help the hiring manager and the new hire prepare. Subsequent sessions take place in the weeks after the start date, with flexibility of timing to suit individual needs.

Onboarding support for the hiring manager may include:

- Reinforcing the importance of helping the new hire to grasp the business and the nuances of the organizational culture, including the unwritten rules
- Examining ways to support the new hire with tactics and strategies for success
- Discussing how the hiring manager can facilitate relationship building across the organization, rather than treating the new hire as a solo performer
- Discussing the appropriate frequency and quality of feedback to ensure clear direction
- Ensuring clear and reasonable expectations and performance metrics for the new hire
- Working through any challenges that may arise in the transition period

Onboarding support for the new hire may include:

- Examining and clarifying the responsibilities of the role and ensuring that the hard-skill and soft-skill expectations are clear

- Devising a plan for learning about the organization—its history, business strategy, culture, and the unwritten rules
- Discussing ways of building effective lines of communication between the new hire and the hiring manager
- Discussing ways of building trust and cooperation across the organization
- Ensuring that the new hire demonstrates true listening, along with the flexibility and adaptability to make any required changes
- Working through any challenges that may arise in the transition period

Because an onboarding program involves coaching for both the hiring manager and the new hire, it addresses challenges from both the organization's and the new hire's perspectives. For example, the program can involve the hiring manager in providing initial information about the organization's unwritten rules. Every organization has its own set of appropriate and inappropriate behaviors. In the absence of guidance, navigating accordingly is fraught with peril for the new hire, who will be grateful for any help in this area.

With the help of the hiring manager, the onboarding program can provide the new hire with guidance on such topics as personal mannerisms, personal space, level of assertiveness, physical presentation, work habits, etiquette, and so on, in relation to the unwritten rules in the organization. In addition, by emphasizing the key fundamental and complementary traits required and discussing them in relation to the position profile, the hiring manager can provide the new hire with invaluable insight into how those traits are related to the behaviors that the organization expects.

The Importance of Ongoing Feedback and Mentoring

Delivering feedback is something that most managers find difficult and shy away from, especially delivering feedback on soft skills. There are many reasons for this, including having concern for the feelings of others or wondering if the issue is important enough to warrant comment. But, as mentioned earlier, if an individual is fired, it's typically because of soft-skill fit issues. So it's critical that, right from the start, new hires receive guidance on how they're fitting in and on how to address any emerging fit issues.

The involvement of both the hiring manager and the new hire in the onboarding program can help set the scene for ongoing support from the manager. For example, giving the new hire advice on the unwritten rules in the organization shouldn't be limited to the onboarding program. Ongoing advice from the hiring manager can include feedback on how the new hire might modify certain behaviors to create a better impression. Since such feedback takes place in the context of encouraging the new hire's successful transition, the hiring manager assumes the role of supporter and mentor and helps create an atmosphere in which ongoing feedback is expected and welcomed, including feedback on soft skills as well as hard skills.

Suppose, for instance, it comes to the manager's attention that the new hire isn't building cross-functional relationships in the way that's expected. Perhaps there have been a few negative comments or just a lack of positive comments. The manager can address the issue right away by having a discussion with the new hire on what the role requires, as described in the position profile, and how communication works best in the organization's culture. The conversation will be about helping the new hire understand organizational norms and providing feedback linked to the responsibilities of the role or the projected career path. The manager might begin a conversation in the following way:

> I think I may be able to help you with one of your responsibilities. As you know, part of your role includes building cross-functional relationships in our collaborative setting. I've noticed that you've been working hard at your desk and that you've not spent much time in other departments. I appreciate your contributions to our department, and I'd like to give you some help in optimizing your relationships across the organization. To gain the respect and cooperation of your peers cross-functionally, I think it's best for you to spend some time with each of the department heads. That way, you can get to know them and their departments and find out what they need from our department. Perhaps I've given you unrealistic deadlines for completing work in our department, or

perhaps there are other reasons that keep you at your desk, so I want to get your thoughts on what support you need to be able to spend more time in other departments.

The hiring manager can provide appropriate support right from the outset by regarding feedback to the new hire as an ongoing responsibility, rather than an occasional task. The manager should avoid waiting weeks or even months for the individual's first performance review to flag areas that require assistance and development. Ongoing feedback and appropriate mentoring work to the advantage of the new hire, the hiring manager, and the organization. Among the other benefits, the *ongoing support provides positive reinforcement to the new hire's decision to accept the job.* The support also conveys the manager's commitment to achievement and results, and it encourages the new hire to contribute fully to the organization. Effective ongoing feedback and mentoring are therefore crucial, not only to optimize performance, increase engagement, and enable professional development, but also to contribute to the retention of valued employees over the longer haul.

The good news for the hiring manager is that, right from the start date, the organization has all the background information needed to support the new hire. The group of interviewers identified the key fit traits required for the role and referred to these traits to screen the successful candidate for the right fit. The prescreening and interviews revealed the new hire's greatest strengths and any significant weaknesses. And the responsibilities of the role, as described in the position profile, incorporate both hard-skill and soft-skill requirements. Ongoing attentiveness to the individual's performance of the role's responsibilities quickly reveals areas in which the new hire needs assistance and further development and allows the hiring manager to pinpoint and provide the needed support.

Performance Reviews

In our career coaching practice, we hear about performance reviews from both the employee's and the employer's points of view. From both sides, we most frequently hear that employees have never had a performance review or that yearly reviews take place but aren't meaningful. In organizations that do conduct performance reviews, the process is often uncomfortable for the managers who deliver the reviews and can also be worrying for employees, who are often unsure of what to expect.

The key to establishing a more positive and productive performance-review process is for the hiring manager to provide the new hire with ongoing feedback and mentoring on both hard and soft skills from day one, as described in the previous section. The performance review is then just an extension of what's already happening. The ongoing feedback typically enhances communication between the hiring manager and the new hire, making the performance review more comfortable for both parties.

Supporting the employee's hard-skill and soft-skill development on an ongoing basis can open up the conversation in the performance review to focus on bigger-picture professional development or career path topics. The performance review can then be more about what the future looks like in terms of the direction of the organization, its future goals, and the impact on the role. There can be discussion around professional development and what the employee can look forward to. In this way, the performance review can positively impact promotions and retention.

If the position profile for the role includes 6-month and 1-year objectives, as we suggested in Chapter 4, they provide a natural starting point for developing a performance-review process.

Long-Term Retention

Many organizations make the mistake of hiring with only their immediate needs in mind, which sets up the distinct possibility of a short-term hire and raises the likelihood of retention problems. However, in using our TAP to screen for both short-term and long-term fit, you're already enabling long-term retention.

A customized and well-designed onboarding program, early mentoring, and supportive feedback solidify the transition of the new hire into the organization, facilitate early success, and lay more groundwork for retention. However, the process doesn't end there. In fact, if retention is important to the organization, the process never ends. Having established and cemented the new hire's fit, the challenge is to nurture and maintain it over the longer term as the organization and the role evolve and the new hire becomes established and devotes more thought to next steps.

Organizations can and do lose talented employees, either quickly or even after many years, through insufficient attention to their need for ongoing challenge and professional development. The vast majority of individuals are motivated by new challenges and learning opportunities and wish to keep energized and stay committed to the organization they work for. In our experience, most individuals would rather stay with their current employer and be challenged than look for a new employer. Devising a customized plan to support ongoing development needs is therefore the final step in the Hiring-for-Fit Checklist in Supplement 1.

Many professional development opportunities are framed in terms of hard skills. There's no doubt that enabling employees to update or expand their hard skills, either through mentoring or more formal instruction, can contribute significantly to staff engagement. However, as in the hiring process, soft skills are often given insufficient attention. If your plan is to build future leadership capacity within your organization and retain your top talent, then it's also prudent to support effective soft-skill development.

One productive way to ensure that your strong performers are positioned for more senior roles in your organization, rather than electing to go elsewhere, is to offer them personalized business coaching on soft-skill development. This coaching can be useful for enhancing critical fundamental traits and for developing the more sophisticated complementary traits needed for success in leadership roles. It's the type of development work that leaders typically ignore, even though their success will largely be based on their soft skills. When coaching is positively positioned as leadership learning, it signals that you're interested in investing in an employee's long-term retention and potential promotion.

By paying for any type of skill development, an employer sends a positive message about its interest in the long-term retention of an employee. *But there's a distinct difference in the outcomes from a general course, designed for a group, and from personalized business coaching, customized to the soft-skill development needs of one individual.* While a general course may impart useful information, it may not precisely address the specific development needs of a particular employee, and it doesn't provide individual feedback to employees about the effectiveness of their own soft skills in the workplace. Personalized business coaching does provide this individual feedback and is especially advantageous when the coaching benefits from the involvement of the hiring manager, working with the coach and the hire toward a common future purpose.

In our experience, the alliance of the hiring manager, the coach, and the hire in career path development sends a very powerful positive message to the hire, who feels acknowledged, respected, and valued and is therefore more committed to the employer. In addition, the hire gains a clearer sense of direction and feels a greater level of control over career prospects. The alliance also serves to enhance open lines of communication, enabling both the hire and the hiring manager to deal more readily with new challenges that the hire may face.

Succession Planning

Over time, all organizations face challenges in replacing key senior employees when they step aside. Finding a suitable replacement in short order can be very difficult for a complex role that may have evolved around the strengths of a particular individual. "Irreplaceable" employees make organizations vulnerable, and undertaking orderly succession planning well in advance can offer protection against undue upheavals.

You will likely find that some employees who were thoroughly screened for fit and who have undergone significant professional development will stand out as perhaps having the potential to advance to very senior roles, maybe even to the top job in the organization. Once you identify an individual as a likely prospect for a *specific* senior role in the future, you must consider the issue of fit *with that role*. You can't assume that the excellent fit of the individual with the present role will automatically ensure fit with the more senior role.

To examine the fit of the individual with the more senior role, you need to analyze the traits that *this role* requires, just as if you were hiring an outside candidate for the role. In doing so, you need to consider the job description for the role, and, of course, you're free to contemplate future changes to the job description that might benefit the organization. Then you must compare the existing traits of the individual with those required for the more senior role. One distinct advantage you have over screening an external candidate is that the internal prospect is already a known quantity in your organization. There is ample opportunity to observe and hear about this individual's traits in action and to develop a very detailed picture of strong and weak traits.

There will almost certainly be differences between the individual's existing traits and those required for fit with the more senior role. The **stretch** that the prospect would need to bridge includes the new or en-hanced traits that the prospect would need to acquire before promotion to the senior role. As with an external hire, you need to consider which of the key traits that need enhancement are coachable. If they're not, or if the individual has shown some resistance to coaching in the past, this person may not be capable of achieving the stretch and may not be a good prospect for the more senior position. If the needed traits are coachable, and the individual is receptive to coaching, you have the opportunity to set up a carefully designed road map for development, specifically geared to succession to the more senior role.

Of course, it's possible that an organization doesn't already have em-ployees with the potential to occupy the most senior roles. In that case, organized succession planning must take a different form, involving ex-ternal hiring. Again, it's risky to try to replace a key senior employee at short notice, so significant forward planning is advisable.

Hiring for fit externally with succession planning in mind adds a level of difficulty to the screening process. There's a difference in hiring a person with the potential for promotion and hiring a person earmarked for a *specific* promotion, especially if it's to a very senior role, such as CEO or President. *If you want to groom an individual for a specific role, then succession planning considerations should be a part of the initial search criteria.*

In addition to considering the skills and traits required for fit with a candidate's initial role, you also need to consider those required for success in the candidate's future, more senior role. When applying our TAP to this special case, you must analyze *both* job descriptions and compare the fundamental and complementary traits required for both roles. And, of course, you need to assess whether the individual is capable of achieving the stretch from the initial role to the more senior role and is motivated to do so. In particular, is the individual receptive to the need for soft-skill, as well as hard-skill, development? And does the individual have the openness to learning that ensures full engagement in the development process? If the answer is yes to both questions, you can set up a road map for development, as you would for an internal prospect.

When hiring externally for succession planning, it's important to consider carefully the anticipated time frame for succession. Hiring a VP to move into a President role requires a different search profile if the succession is to occur in 2 years, rather than 5 years. The different time frame for learning will impact the skills you need the candidate to have at the time of the hire. A grooming period of only 2 years will require a closer initial match to the hard-skill and soft-skill requirements of the President role. And because the different time frames will appeal to candidates with different motivation and expectations, there will be an effect on who will genuinely want the role.

In our management consulting and executive search practices, we work with our clients to map out their succession-planning needs. If the right people have been hired for long-term fit in the first place, and personalized development plans have been implemented, then promoting internal successors to the top roles is associated with lower risk than going outside.

Keeping outstanding employees for the long term and benefiting from their advancement require active decisions to hire the right fit at the outset and to provide the right follow-through on long-term development. By establishing, maintaining, and enhancing fit, you can remove the common frustrations involved in hiring, including the underperformance and high turnover that lead to repeated refilling of the same position. By hiring and nurturing the right fit, you can work with outstanding people who want a long-term association with your organization, who represent a great return on your investment, and who grow into the leadership roles that will take your company into the next stage of growth.

Fit in Action: Retaining and Advancing the Right Hire

For one of my searches, I was tasked to find the next superstar sales executive for a very fast-growing company. This was a critical hire. Although the company had a large sales team, only a handful were high producers, and two of those were about to retire. The company's future success depended heavily on hiring new sales associates with exceptional potential who could become high producers and would be motivated to stay and advance with the company over the long haul.

I talked to the President and senior members of the sales team to understand the requirements of the role. For anyone joining the company, there was a long ramp-up period, as the sales cycle was complex. The company wanted to hire an individual with star potential, someone at an early career stage who had demonstrated exceptional ability, but who wasn't too entrenched in a current role. The hope was that the individual would be ready to make a move for the right position, since he or she wouldn't have invested many years in establishing a client base. The role would be presented as a long-term career opportunity with mentoring, career development, and upward mobility, together with the potential for outstanding compensation over the longer term.

We talked at length about the traits that a new hire would need for the initial role and to succeed long term. To understand the long-term requirements, we analyzed the traits of the company's top senior sales executive who had been with the company for many years. This top performer was strong in a number of fundamental traits: work ethic, friendliness, interest in others, persistence, diligence, resilience, humility, will to succeed, results-orientation, writing ability, and articulateness. Strong complementary traits included ability to cope with high pressure, advanced relationship-management ability, advanced listening ability, negotiation ability, initiative, entrepreneurial outlook, business acumen, customer-service focus, and polished presence.

In the search process, we concentrated on screening for the necessary fundamental traits and for such complementary traits as initiative and entrepreneurial outlook that a suitable candidate at an early career stage might have. We also screened for the potential to develop the more sophisticated complementary traits, such as advanced relationship-management ability, to ensure long-term fit with the client's needs. Since the company was planning extensive professional development to retain and promote the individual over the long term, we looked for openness to change, openness to feedback, and openness to learning to ensure readiness for coaching over the coming years.

The extensive screening resulted in the company hiring an outstanding individual who was ready for a steep learning curve, enjoyed and valued the training and mentoring provided, and felt that she'd joined a company that was looking out for her best interests, in both the short and long term. And the effective screening and development processes established a way of recruiting top talent into similar roles and provided a solid foundation for retention and succession planning.

Supplement 1:
Hiring-for-Fit Checklist

Tracking steps in the Trait Alignment Protocol

Key steps in hiring for fit	Completed
1. Prepare a draft overview of the role.	
2. Finalize the selection of interviewers.	
3. Obtain a commitment from all interviewers to the hiring timelines.	
4. Build key fundamental and complementary traits lists for the role.	
5. Transform the draft overview into a position profile.	
6. Establish compensation range, career path, location, and work demands.	
7. Conduct a thorough prescreening of candidates.	
8. Use an interviewing approach that focuses on fit.	
9. Ensure compatibility between candidate expectations and the role.	
10. For senior roles, ensure thorough screening for fundamental traits.	
11. Conduct interviews so that the true character of each candidate emerges.	
12. Reach a well-founded consensus on candidate fit.	
13. Ensure a smooth transition for the new hire through onboarding coaching.	
14. Use the position profile as a basis for ongoing feedback and performance reviews.	
15. Devise a customized plan to support ongoing development needs.	

Supplement 2: Fundamental Traits List

Productivity

Accountability

Accuracy

Analytical ability

Can-do attitude

Commitment to quality

Decision-making ability

Dependability

Determination

Diligence

Efficiency

Hard-working approach

Logical mindset

Persistence

Responsibility

Responsiveness

Results-orientation

Thoroughness

Timeliness

Will to succeed

Work ethic

Self-management

Ability to balance work and rest

Ability to deal with stress

Ability to manage emotions

Calmness

Energy level

Focus

Follow-through

Integrity
Judgment
Organizational ability
Punctuality
Resilience
Respect for physical boundaries
Self-awareness
Self-control
Self-discipline
Self-respect
Time-management ability
Understanding one's impact on others

Relationship building
Ability to build rapport
Appreciativeness
Cooperativeness
Empathy
Enthusiasm
Fairness
Friendliness
Gratitude
Helpfulness
Honesty
Humility
Humor
Interest in others
Loyalty
Patience
Politeness
Positive attitude
Reasonableness
Respect for the opinions of others
Sense of business etiquette
Sense of social etiquette
Sincerity

Straightforwardness

Team-orientation

Warmth

Willingness to share information

Presentation

Ability to ask the right questions

Ability to deliver relevant information

Ability to engage the listener

Acknowledgment of others

Articulateness

Attention to detail

Awareness of clothing and grooming

Awareness of nonverbal messages

Awareness of personal space

Awareness of verbal messages

Coherence

Confidence

Level of formality

Listening ability

Respect for confidentiality

Speed of communication

Voice tone, pitch, and quality

Writing ability

Open Mindset

Acceptance

Adaptability

Curiosity

Flexibility

Humility

Interest in learning from others

Openness to change

Openness to feedback

Openness to learning

Tolerance

Supplement 3:
Complementary Traits List

Ability to ask open-ended questions
Ability to cope with high pressure
Ability to deal with ambiguity
Ability to delegate
Ability to establish credibility
Ability to motivate others
Ability to think outside the box
Advanced decision-making ability
Advanced listening ability
Advanced problem-solving ability
Advanced quality focus
Advanced relationship-management ability
Assertiveness
Autonomy
Business acumen
Change-catalyst capacity
Charisma
Collaborative approach
Commitment to business ethics
Conflict-management ability
Continuous-improvement outlook
Creativity
Customer-service focus
Decisiveness
Diplomacy
Drive for results
Dynamism
Enjoyment of challenge
Entrepreneurial outlook

Facilitation ability
Forward-thinking ability
Independence
Influencing ability
Initiative
Innovation
Insight
Intellectual capacity
Interpersonal savvy
Intuition
Leadership presence
Managerial courage
Mentoring capacity
Meticulousness
Negotiation ability
Open communication style
Optimism
Perceptiveness
Persuasiveness
Planning ability
Polished presence
Political savvy
Priority-setting ability
Process-improvement outlook
Realism
Resourcefulness
Self-development capacity
Stamina
Strategic agility
Vision
Willingness to take calculated risks

Supplement 4:
Table 3.1 Recording and Rating Fundamental Traits

	Strong								Weak	
Productivity	10	9	8	7	6	5	4	3	2	1
Trait										
Trait										
Trait										

	Strong								Weak	
Self-management	10	9	8	7	6	5	4	3	2	1
Trait										
Trait										
Trait										

	Strong								Weak	
Relationship building	10	9	8	7	6	5	4	3	2	1
Trait										
Trait										
Trait										

	Strong								Weak	
Presentation	10	9	8	7	6	5	4	3	2	1
Trait										
Trait										
Trait										

	Strong								Weak	
Open mindset	10	9	8	7	6	5	4	3	2	1
Trait										
Trait										
Trait										

Supplement 5:
Table 3.3 Recording and Rating Complementary Traits

	Strong								Weak	
	10	9	8	7	6	5	4	3	2	1
Trait										
Trait										
Trait										
Trait										
Trait										
Trait										
Trait										
Trait										
Trait										
Trait										
Trait										
Trait										
Trait										
Trait										
Trait										

About the Author

For more than 30 years, **Janet Webb** has tracked and advanced the careers of professionals, becoming a recognized expert in executive search, outplacement, career and business coaching, and hiring-related management consulting. She has acquired a detailed understanding of the hiring criteria and practices in all major industry sectors, including financial services, manufacturing, retail, real estate, mining, high-tech, health care, and not-for-profit. She has worked closely with a wide range of leaders, from CEOs to line managers, in a wide range of functional areas, including finance, operations, human resources, systems, sales, and administration.

Janet founded JW Associates International Inc. in Toronto, Canada, in 2003 to bring together two elements: a passion for conducting high-quality retained executive searches and a commitment to supporting leaders in optimizing their careers. The focus at JW Associates has been to understand fully the concept of fit from both the client's and the candidate's perspectives.

Before founding JW Associates, Janet was a Partner at the search firm Lannick Associates in Toronto. She began her career as a teacher, having obtained her Bachelor of Education degree, with honors, from the University of Alberta.

Janet's speaking engagements have included workshops for Fortune 500 companies on retention and hiring challenges and presentations to CEOs, HR professionals, and recruiters on how to hire, retain, and advance top talent. She has also worked with growing companies on organizational structure and design and on building high-performing teams.

Janet has self-published two books. *Interview to Offer: The Definitive Guide to Establishing Fit and Landing the Job,* published in e-book format in 2011, provides practical and effective guidance to candidates on demonstrating fit in an interview. *Hiring for Keeps: How to Hire Outstanding Employees Who Fit, Stay and Add to the Bottom Line,* published in print and e-book formats in 2015, provides insight on hiring for fit. She distributed this book in Canada, where the *Globe and Mail* named it as one of the Top 10 Leadership and Management Books of 2015.

In 2018, Janet was recognized as one of the top three finalists in the Talent Catalyst category of the Toronto Region Board of Trade's 8th Annual Business Excellence Awards.

Janet's current focus is on consulting with leaders through her management consulting practice in order to share the ideas described in the present book, *Hiring for Fit: A Key Leadership Skill.*

Index

OTHER TITLES IN THE HUMAN RESOURCE MANAGEMENT AND ORGANIZATIONAL BEHAVIOR COLLECTION

- *Practicing Management* by Alan S. Gutterman
- *Practicing Leadership* by Alan S. Gutterman
- *Women Leaders: The Power of Working Abroad* by Sapna Welsh and Caroline Kersten
- *Breakthrough: Career Strategies for Women's Success* by Saundra Stroope
- *Comparative Management Studies* by Alan S. Gutterman
- *Cross-Cultural Leadership Studies* by Alan S.Gutterman
- *No Cape Required: Empowering Abundant Leadership* by Bob Hughes and Helen Caton Hughes
- *Leading Organizational Transformation* by Linda Mattingly
- *Transforming the Next Generation Leaders* by Sattar Bawany
- *Chief Kickboxing Officer: Applying the Fight Mentality to Business Success* by Alfonso Asensio
- *Untenable: A Leader's Guide to Addressing the Big Issues That Are Ignored, Falsely Explained, or Inappropriately Tolerated* by Gary Covert
- *The Relevance of Humanities to the 21st Century Workplace* by Michael Edmondson
- *Uniquely Great: Essentials for Winning Employers* by Lucy English
- *Successful Recruitment: How to Recruit the Right People For Your Business* by Stephen Amos
- *Level-Up Leadership: Engaging Leaders for Success* by Michael J. Proverita

Announcing the Business Expert Press Digital Library

Concise e-books business students need for classroom and research

This book can also be purchased in an e-book collection by your library as

- *a one-time purchase,*
- *that is owned forever,*
- *allows for simultaneous readers,*
- *has no restrictions on printing, and*
- *can be downloaded as PDFs from within the library community.*

Our digital library collections are a great solution to beat the rising cost of textbooks. E-books can be loaded into their course management systems or onto students' e-book readers. The **Business Expert Press** digital libraries are very affordable, with no obligation to buy in future years. For more information, please visit **www.businessexpertpress.com/librarians**. To set up a trial in the United States, please email **sales@businessexpertpress.com**.